CELEBRATING
OKLAHOMA!

CELEBRATING
OKLAHOMA!
THE OKLAHOMA CENTENNIAL
PHOTOGRAPHIC SURVEY

Mike Klemme

ISBN (Special Edition)   978-0-941233-01-9
ISBN (Collectors Edition)   978-0-941233-02-6

Library of Congress Control Number 2007929251

For orders, reorders or related products, see www.celebratingoklahoma.com.

Design by Source Publications, Inc., Tulsa, OK, www.sourcepub.com.

Printed in the United States of America by Consolidated Printing Solutions, Tulsa OK, www.cpsolutions.biz.

TABLE OF CONTENTS

Brad Henry
Office of the Governor
State of Oklahoma

 Oklahoma's 100th birthday is an opportunity to showcase and celebrate the beauty, energy and joy that define our state. Fortunately, the book you now hold in your hands is an outstanding way to do just that.

 Over the course of 20 months, Mike Klemme, the official photographer of the Oklahoma Centennial, traveled thousands of miles visiting every nook and cranny of Oklahoma, capturing with his camera the very best that our state has to offer. In this endeavor, Mike collaborated with a team of talented writers to tell the stories behind many of those pictures.

 As Governor of this great state, it is my pleasure to introduce you to *Celebrating Oklahoma!* On these pages, friends near and far can revel in some of the grandeur and excitement of Oklahoma. Many of these images are certain to rekindle fond memories for longtime Oklahomans. Others are bound to be enchanted by this sweeping view of the Oklahoma experience.

 And, by all means, keep this special volume handy. It will be an excellent reference the next time you want to tell someone else about the diversity, beauty and vitality that is Oklahoma!

THE ART OF *SEEING*

by Mike Klemme

Every journey starts with an initial spark.

The spark that began my photographic journey was a special Christmas gift in 1959 when I was just six years old. My sweet grandmother gave me a simple envelope containing a gift card for a subscription to *National Geographic*, along with my first issue of the magazine. To this day, I still remember the cover of that first issue—an illustration of space in recognition of the launch of Sputnik.

Clissie Klemme, Mike's Grandmother (1976)

I might as well have been on the launching pad with that famous satellite because the magazine's contents sent me reeling. I remember the thrill of ripping the brown paper off each new issue to discover which exotic lands were featured that month. Little did I know that as I was learning about the world, I was also learning to see beauty—through the eyes of some of the most fantastic photographers of our time.

If my grandmother's gift was the spark, my dad was the engine that drove my passion.

As a child, I dreamed of becoming an architect. Not just an Enid architect drawing up house plans, but a New York architect designing skyscrapers. Someone like Frank Lloyd Wright—a visionary who thought outside of the box and created controversial designs. Like many young boys, a good portion of my summers were spent at the pool and the ballpark, but my dad's workshop was an equally special place. There, Dad taught me to draw six-view perspectives and obliques by cutting wooden blocks into intricate shapes, which I would then spend hours drawing.

Bob and Doris Klemme, Mike's parents (1976)

My dreams of being an architect faded—math was not my strong suit! However, the lessons I learned from drawing those blocks not only survived but grew. I learned to see things from every angle, to look at an object until its true essence became clear, and to realize that every person and thing possesses beauty. You just have to dig deeper with some.

Always proud to be from Oklahoma! (1963)

If Grandma was the spark and Dad was the engine, Mom provided the fuel. Most people from reasonably happy families will claim that their mother was or is the most wonderful, sweet, selfless and supportive person on earth. I am here to tell you that my mom won the award! No matter what I did, Mom was behind me 150 percent. She was my biggest fan and gave me the self-esteem to take on any challenge. I miss her every day, and wish that she could hold this book in her hands and read these words.

The Art of Traveling

My parents also introduced me to the joys and value of travel. While I yearned to have a brother or sister, being an only child did make it easier for my family to take off on short getaways. We enjoyed countless Sunday afternoon drives to Woolaroc, Salt Plains, Flint Creek, Roman Nose State Park and Red Rock Canyon. And day trips to hunt, picnic,

fish, look for rocks or visit relatives around the state. All gave me a great appreciation for Oklahoma and its bounties—an appreciation that has stayed with me through my life.

Each year, the Klemme family also took a two-week summer vacation. Before departure, Dad would show me the route he had marked out—explaining where we would camp, and what monuments and national parks we were about to see. We drove to places like Colorado, Utah, Texas, New Mexico, Arizona and South Dakota. When I was 10, we drove to the World's Fair in Seattle via Glacier National Park, Banff and the Canadian Rockies.

The year of my 13th birthday, I began bugging Dad about New York City. I wanted to see the big city and watch the God-like New York Yankees (especially fellow Oklahoman Mickey Mantle) play in their home stadium. Dad replied, "You plan the trip and we will go."

I began planning a route that would take us not only through New York City, but also St. Louis, Chicago, Detroit and Washington, D.C. I wrote the chambers of commerce in each city and town along the way, asking for information—literally hundreds of letters. I can still remember walking barefoot each day to the post office about a mile from our house. My excitement grew as more and more of the chambers responded. By the end of the summer, I had meticulously planned every stop on our New York adventure and secured hotel reservations for each night of the trip.

One day, like a gift from above, my monthly *National Geographic* issue arrived—with a map of Manhattan! A map that showed every street, major building, park and monument on the island. Enough detail for me to practically memorize the city before we visited. I became the virtual tour guide for Mom and Dad.

Two Passions Collide

Several years later, I headed off to college where, as Jackson Browne said, "...you meet the fools that a young fool meets." Fortunately, this young fool met a friend who shared a book of photography by Edward Weston. Weston had a peculiarly artistic way of looking at common things, such as green peppers, bedpans and rocks. I was completely taken by these black-and-white images, and years later studied Weston's life and body of work in earnest.

Shooting at Salt Plains National Wildlife Refuge (1978)

I came out of college wondering how I could possibly use what I had learned. For me, the first step was moving back home to sell advertising for the *Enid News and Eagle*. There, two of my best friends, Jerry Nickell and Tom Taylor, were amateur photographers. They often invited me along on their weekend excursions to photograph wildlife. During one of those trips, Jerry asked if I would

Klemme at the **Enid News and Eagle** *(1979)*

like to look through the viewfinder of his camera. The moment I did, I felt as if I were doing something for which I had trained my entire life. A whole new world opened up through that small hole.

I soon bought a Nikomat EL from a mail-order company in China along with a couple of lenses. My photographic life had begun. For fun, I began making weekly trips to wildlife refuges. But the ad salesman in me also figured out that if I took a few good photos of my

clients' stores or products, they would run larger ads. I became the number-one salesperson at the paper and was rapidly building quite a portfolio of commercial photography—which helped me land a job as a photographer/designer at Liberty National Bank in Oklahoma City. (It also gave me the distinct pleasure of seeing my work in print—something I still enjoy to this day.)

Then came a crystallizing moment. Tom Taylor was hired as the assistant golf pro at a new golf course and real estate development in Edmond, called Oak Tree Country Club. The director of golf was an old friend and fraternity brother named Steve Braley. Steve said he had heard I was doing photography and wondered if I would take some photographs to sell real estate around the course.

Of course, I said yes. Soon my photos were in Oak Tree's brochures, tournament programs, posters and clubhouse. Other assignments with other clubs soon followed.

Still eager to learn, I enrolled in a one-week class at Quartz Mountain Institute. One of the instructors, Phillip Hyde, was a master landscape artist whose work I had long admired in Sierra Club calendars and books. The other instructor was a former *National Geographic* guy named Dick Durrance who worked worldwide for clients like Marlboro and Kool cigarettes.

Each day of class, Phillip and Dick organized a photography contest. I won every one. Dick and I also connected personally. I spent hours bugging him with questions about the business side of photography. I also shared my dream of shooting golf courses for real-estate developers. On the last day of the class, he looked me in the eye and said, "You need to quit your job and do photography full time!" I spent the four-hour drive home trying to decide how to persuade my wife, Suzanne, that I should leave the bank to photograph golf courses full time. That night, when I told her what I was thinking, she instantly responded, "Let's do it!"

I will love her for all eternity if for no other reason than that single moment.

Students at the Quartz Mountain Institute (1984)

Suzanne and I decided that if I was going to travel for a living, we should live in Enid so our children could be raised in the same nurturing environment we had known. Living in Enid may have complicated my travel arrangements over the years, but it allowed the kids to grow up around their grandparents and in a community we love.

Over the next 25 years, I traveled more than 4 million miles to shoot 1,700 golf courses in 45 countries—including places like Augusta National, St. Andrews, Doral, Pinehurst, Cypress Point and Oakmont. I loved the travel, but I hated being away from my family for so many weeks each year. Even so, golf course photography put groceries on the table, and allowed me to take Suzanne and the kids to great places, hopefully spawning a new generation of travelers.

The Klemme kids, from left: Paige, Brett and Ryan (1991)

I now have friends all over the United States and the world. My camera has taken me behind the gates of some of the world's most exclusive destinations and allowed me to stay at many of the planet's plushest resorts. I have dined in palaces with dukes, met kings of industry, and worked alongside legends of the game like Palmer, Nicklaus, Player, Weiskopf and Crenshaw. I have worked on two major books with the prestigious publisher Harry N. Abrams in New York—*Grand Slam Golf* by George Peper and *Golf Resorts of the World* by Brian McCallen. Since 1990, I also have been honored to serve on the *Golf Magazine* panel to select the Top 100 Golf Courses in the World and the Top 100 Golf Courses in the United States.

Santa Fe Workshop

In the summer of 1996, I attended a workshop in Santa Fe led by another *National Geographic* photographer, Sam Abell. His class, The Project Workshop, showed students how to create, develop and execute ideas for long-term photographic book projects. I went into the class contemplating some sort of large project based on golf images. But another idea began to take shape—a photography book for Oklahoma's upcoming 100th birthday.

Over the course of several months, I pieced together a plan to document the state for our Centennial. In preparation, I studied how my favorite photographers, such as Weston, Ansel Adams and Paul Strand, had tackled their own documentary photo projects at some point in their careers.

The Project

In *Celebrating Oklahoma!*, my hope is to capture the essence of life in Oklahoma. Where we are today and how we are positioned to grow into the future. Artistic landscapes revealing the diverse landforms in our state. Documentary photographs showing the resilience of our people, our pioneer spirit and our self-sufficiency.

Wade Hampton Golf Club, Cashiers, N.C. (1990)

Lake Murray, Oklahoma (2007)

More than anything, I want to boost our state's self-confidence. My hope is that *Celebrating Oklahoma!* will be purchased as a gift and passed down from generation to generation—and that Oklahoma-based companies will use the book to recruit customers and employees. But most of all, I hope this book will convince young Oklahomans of the great opportunities in our state.

For years, thousands of our young people have worked their way through Oklahoma's education system only to move away for what they perceive as greater opportunities elsewhere. Through these photographs, perhaps our youth will realize that Oklahoma is an amazing place full of opportunities as wonderful as those found anywhere. Why not be successful here at home?

I began taking these pictures in September of 2005 and completed the photographs on April 15, 2007. A mere 20 months to complete what literally could have been a lifetime of work. I can't count the number of times I had only three hours to shoot a location that deserved several weeks. It was painful to decide which sites or festivals I simply didn't have time to attend. Even so, I visited every corner of our state and did my very best to include as many highlights as possible.

In closing, I want to thank my terrific partners in this endeavor. Thanks to Carl Renfro and his wife, Carolyn, from Ponca City, without whose help this project would have never happened on this scale. I also want to thank Jim Trecek and his wife, Barbara. Jim's vast business expertise gave the venture a firm financial and operational foundation. And the Treceks couldn't have been more gracious in opening their Tulsa home to me so many times over the past two years. Rick Long and the Source Publications team did a fabulous job with the writing, design and production on the book, our Web site (www.celebratingoklahoma.com), and our marketing materials. Thanks also to Margaret Wright, who has been my right hand through this and other projects during the past 18 years. Finally, to my number-one partner, my wife Suzanne, who served as bookkeeper, salesperson and chief psychologist for the project: I love you with all of my heart—thanks for putting up with me the past 25 years!

Enough of all of this, let's get on with the book.
And let's Celebrate Oklahoma!

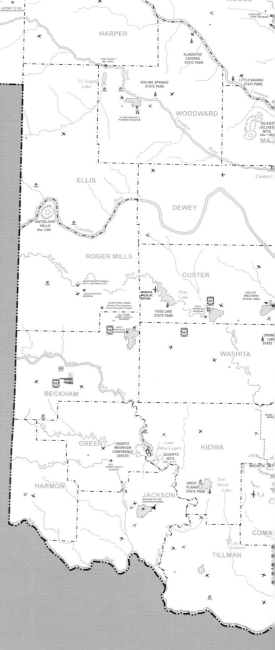

THE GREAT STATE OF
OKLAHOMA

This map of our great state—courtesy of The Oklahoma Department of
Transportation—shows the location of each of our 77 counties, as well as
state parks and other major points of interest.

For a city-by-city listing of all photographs in *Celebrating Oklahoma!*,
see the index beginning on page 284.

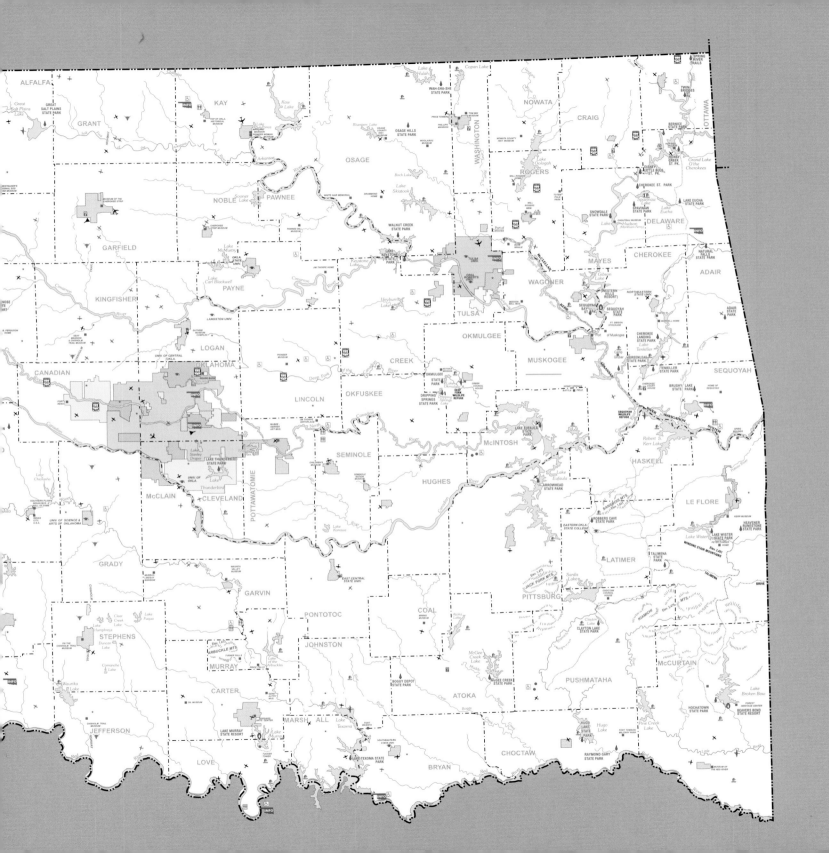

LAND

A Grand Land, Indeed!

In two simple lines, Oklahoma's Official State Song succinctly sums up what many Oklahomans feel about their state:

> **"We know we belong to the land.**
> **And the land we belong to is grand!"**

The story of Oklahoma—and Oklahomans—begins with a land that certainly is grand. From the lush green hills of northeastern Oklahoma and the dramatic mountain ranges on the state's southeastern boundary to the undisturbed grass

prairies in the middle and the vibrantly tinted mesas in the west, Oklahoma holds grand surprises at every turn.

But "grand" only begins to describe what makes this place so special. So unique. So completely unexpected.

Oklahoma's natural landscapes take visitors by surprise. Especially those visitors who picture the arid place so memorably described as a "Dust Bowl" all those years ago. But this former "Dust Bowl" is anything but dry or dusty today.

Oklahoma is home to more than 1 million surface acres of freshwater lakes, ponds, rivers and streams, not to mention tree-topped mountain ranges and seemingly endless swatches of prairie grasses.

This diversity of terrain is a surprise, even to those who call this state home. Many are surprised to learn that Oklahoma has 12 distinct ecoregions (or types of terrain). That's more per square mile than any other state in the nation.

These ecoregions run the gamut from rocky mountain foothills to hardwood forests to cypress swamps, and allow visitors and residents alike the ability to experience almost every type of outdoor activity within the borders of one state.

The prairie terrain is a good place to start uncovering Oklahoma's authentic treasures. Oklahomans are working hard to preserve those shortgrass, mixed-grass and tallgrass

1 Mesa, Glass Mountains, FAIRVIEW

3 Oklahoma Sky, STRONG CITY

2 Mt. Scott, Lake Ellsworth, LAWTON

4 Boulders, Wichita Mountain Wildlife Refuge, INDIAHOMA

prairies that escaped the settlers' plows, and to restore others lost to urban sprawl and conversion to cropland. The Tallgrass Prairie Preserve in northern Oklahoma, for example, is the largest protected remnant of tallgrass prairie left on earth. Now home to free-roaming bison, this fully functioning prairie ecosystem encourages people to value "the way things were" and the way things can be in the future.

At the other end of the spectrum are the forests that cover nearly a quarter of the state's territory. The Ouachita National Forest, the south's oldest and largest national forest, is home to wildlife, tall pines and more than 700 miles of trails.

But Oklahoma is much more than grass and trees. For a state that is considered part of the Great Plains, Oklahoma is anything but flat. The state's four mountain ranges are a testament to that.

One of the best ways to immerse yourself in Oklahoma's mountainous scenery is to jump in a car and travel the Talimena Scenic Drive, a 55-mile route that clings to the top of Winding Stair Mountain in the southeastern part of the state.

Visitors may also be surprised by western Oklahoma's rough and rugged canyons and mesas of red, green and yellow—scenery that one would more likely expect to find in the Badlands than in the Heartland.

The natural variety of Oklahoma's land tells only part of the story, however. The state's landscape is truly defined by its many rivers, lakes and streams.

And "many" merely hints at the wealth of our water features. In fact, Oklahoma contains more miles of shoreline than the Atlantic and Gulf Coasts combined. These shorelines wind around some surprisingly diverse bodies of water.

The 22-mile-long Broken Bow Lake at Beavers Bend State Park in southeastern Oklahoma, for example, has water so clear that scuba divers train there. And a little further north, Lake Tenkiller is home to an underwater scuba park that offers

1 Navajo Mountains, HEADRICK

3 Waterfall, MEDICINE PARK

2 Sycamore Leaf Floats on Water, Falls Creek, DAVIS

LAND 🌳 ⛰️

challenging dives in 200 old homesites that became submerged during the formation of the lake.

Those who venture to the saltwater lake at Great Salt Plains State Park in northwestern Oklahoma might want to trade air tanks for binoculars, as this area's white, salt-covered sand and shallow salty lakes are critical habitats for many bird species.

Oklahoma is also home to natural landforms without equal. Towering gypsum bluffs and the largest public gypsum cave in the world are found at Alabaster Caverns State Park in the state's northwest region.

The hilly woodlands of the San Bois Mountains in southeast Oklahoma contain both beautiful and

historic landforms. This rugged area was inhabited first by ancient peoples and more recently by "Wild West" outlaws. Some of Oklahoma's most colorful history was created here when Jesse James and his gang hid out in what is now known as Robbers Cave State Park.

Nature's handiwork is also evident in the ever-changing sand dunes in northwestern Oklahoma. More than 1,000 acres of rideable dunes range in height from 25 to 75 feet and change shape upon the whim of the winds each day.

The past still speaks loudly at Black Mesa, the state's highest elevation (at 4,973 feet above sea level), where you can literally

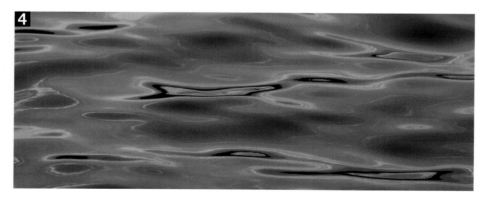

1 Flint Creek, near KANSAS

3 Prairie, HARMON

2 American Lotus, Woolaroc, BARTLESVILLE

4 Rippling Water, Grand Lake O' the Cherokees, GROVE

walk in the steps of the dinosaurs. Dinosaur tracks are visible in solid rock in a creek bed near the base of the mesa.

The past can be experienced throughout the state's landscapes, most notably in Cimarron County, where a trail used by Native Americans, scouts and trappers to cross the southern plains long before wagon traffic is still visible.

Oklahomans continue to leave their mark in the landscape, even if today's trails take a decidedly more modern slant. The McClellan-Kerr Navigation System in northeastern Oklahoma is a perfect example. This navigable waterway connects Oklahoma to the Gulf of Mexico and

shows how Oklahomans continue to define themselves by how they belong to the water and land.

Mountains. Rivers. Old-growth forests. Canyons. Salt flats. Cypress swamps. Prairies. Oklahoma has them all and so much more. Yes, this is a grand land.

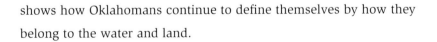

1 Spider in the Dew, WILBURTON

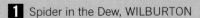
3 Arkansas River, CLEVELAND

2 Altus-Lugart Lake, ALTUS

4 Wild Flora, TULSA

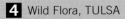

Sunrise, ERICK ■

The pink-carpeted sky glows over the prairie to mark the end of a day in Erick—a town filled with historic downtown buildings, as well as plenty of space to enjoy nature's beauty.

■ **Red Rock Canyon State Park, HINTON**

This canyon, located just south of Hinton, was formed by streams rushing past the ancient red rocks of the area. The 310-acre state park is usually populated with rappellers, hikers and adventurers of all sorts.

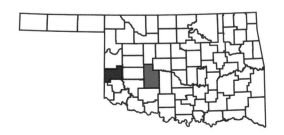

My great grandparents settled in this area before the Civil War. Owning a portion of that original place is most important to our love of the land. Donna and I cherish the legacy of both being "true Oklahomans." It's truly something to celebrate!

— CLEM McSPADDEN
Oklahoma U.S. Representative, 1973-1975

■ **Cornstalks, BILLINGS**
Cornstalks reach for the clouds in Billings, located in Noble County.

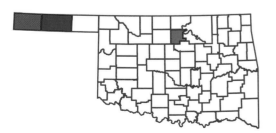

Sunflowers, TYRONE ■
These spent blooms grace the roadside in the panhandle town of Tyrone.

■ **Black Mesa Morning, KENTON**

Sky and hills combine to form the canvas for this sunrise scene. The orange sky hosts puffs of dark clouds, reminiscent of smoke signals. Standing at 4,973 feet, Black Mesa is the highest point in Oklahoma.

DID YOU KNOW? Per square mile, Oklahoma contains more eco-regions (12) than any other state in the country.

Alligator, Red Slough Wildlife Management Area, IDABEL
This alligator is one in a population of 10 that live among 5,814 acres of wetlands. The area is designed to restore hydrology and re-establish bottomland hardwoods.

Tallgrass Prairie Preserve, PAWHUSKA ■

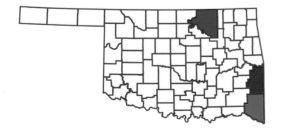

■ Channel Dam, COWLINGTON
This lock and dam system is an architectural marvel
spanning the McClellan-Kerr Navigational Channel.

■ **Cattails, JET**
These cattails are prevalent around the ponds and marshes at Salt Plains National Wildlife Refuge, established in 1930.

Rock Formations, Black Mesa State Park, KENTON ■
Distinctive free-standing rock formations and assorted plant life are all part of hikers' enjoyment at Black Mesa State Park.

■ **Broken Bow River, Beavers Bend State Park, BROKEN BOW**
This stream spills into Broken Bow Lake. It's a perfect place for a day of fly-fishing.

Grazing Goats, ADA ■

Goat farms are located throughout Oklahoma. This small
herd enjoys an afternoon snack of prairie grass.

■ Sunset, Lake Ellsworth, LAWTON
Mt. Sheridan's silhouette stands out against the sunset canvas.

Prairie Dog, Wichita Mountain Wildlife Refuge, INDIAHOMA

Prairie dogs now flourish in three areas of the refuge, which specializes in introducing and preserving species historically native to the area. Other animals include buffalo, longhorn cattle, river otters and burrowing owls.

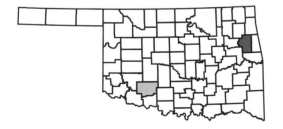

> **B**eginning with the land run, Oklahoma has a spirit like no other state in America ... it's the diamond in the heartland.
>
> — JEANNE TRIPPLEHORN
> *Actress*

Fall, TAHLEQUAH
Fall foliage delights the eye with yellows and oranges in the rolling hills of the Oklahoma Ozarks.

Windmill, ENID ■
Only the most serene evening can create such a scene as this vintage Oklahoma windmill at sunset.

■ **Robbers Cave State Park, WILBURTON**
Early morning fog rises in Robbers Cave State Park, revealing the San Bois Mountains in the background.

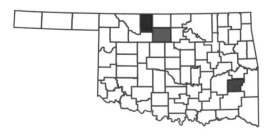

As a third-generation Oklahoman, I have never really had an urge to live anywhere other than Oklahoma. Being an artist I guess I could have moved anywhere in the world, but I have always felt connected to the land and people of Oklahoma. I don't think you can find a more generous, hard-working, honest or decent group of folks than Oklahomans.

— **HAROLD (H.T.) HOLDEN**
Artist

■ Salt Fork of the Arkansas River, NESCATUNGA

The Salt Fork of the Arkansas River glows at sunset. Salt Fork, also known as "Nescatunga," meaning "Big Salt Water," is a 192-mile tributary that was dammed to form the Great Salt Plains Lake in Alfalfa County.

Maize Field, near FORGAN ■

■ **North Canadian River, HARMON**
A view of the vast North Canadian River Valley outside of Harmon in Ellis County.

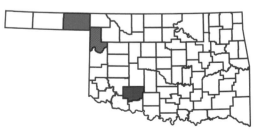

■ **Bison, Wichita Mountain Wildlife Refuge, INDIAHOMA**
An average of 600 American bison roam free on the Wichita Mountain grasslands.

■ Glass Mountains, FAIRVIEW

This mesa in Glass Mountain State Park is located outside of Fairview in the heart of a chain of flat-top mesas that run across western Major County.

> **W**hen you cast your eyes across the vividly hued, richly textured Oklahoma landscape, you glimpse the majesty with which the Creator expresses itself. No wonder Native American thought had no concept for man owning this land. It is impossible for ego to personally hoard or hold magnificence. Indeed, we belong to this land.
>
> — ALFRE WOODARD
> *Oscar-nominated actress*

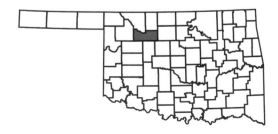

Ouachita National Forest, TALIHINA ■
Talimena Scenic Drive is a 54-mile stretch of Oklahoma road, designated a National Scenic Byway. A leisurely drive or hike gives visitors an up-close look at nature through the changing seasons.

■ **Grain Silos, FORGAN**
Silos stand in formation in the sunlight outside of Forgan.

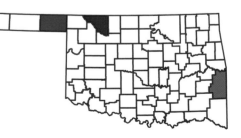

■ **Salt Pans, FREEDOM**
The Cargill Salt Pans, located just west of Freedom, are where the Cimarron River created one of Oklahoma's largest natural salt deposits.

■ Arkansas River, CLEVELAND

■ Glass Mountains, **FAIRVIEW**

DID YOU KNOW? Made possible by political efforts of U.S. presidents McKinley and Roosevelt, establishment of the Wichita Mountain Wildlife Refuge paved the way for the National Wildlife Refuge System in America.

Lily Pad, IDABEL ■
The afternoon sun casts long shadows in interesting patterns on the broad green leaf of this lily pad.

■ **Hay Bales, HOOKER**
These round hay bales offer a good square meal to grazing livestock in the small town of Hooker.

■ Dunes, Little Sahara Park, WAYNOKA

This "little" park is full of big adventure, with more than 1,600 acres of sand dunes. Some reach heights of 75 feet, and all are perfect for riding.

When I think of Oklahoma, I become enormously proud that it is my home. As Sooners, our personal relationships are somehow more close-knit because of our shared frontier heritage, that red dirt, and the wondrous beauty and vastness of this spectacular land.

— BARRY L. SWITZER
Head football coach, University of Oklahoma, 1973-1988

Snow on Pod, near CHEROKEE ■

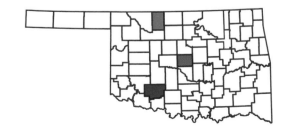

■ **Thistle Detail, EDMOND**

This dried thistle pod, with its wispy feathered strands, spores
in the fall to produce a full-grown thistle bloom each summer.

■ **Creek, MEERS**

This creek runs to the Wichita Mountains in Meers—a town founded in 1902 by gold miners.

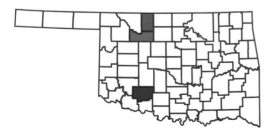

Plowed Field, CHEROKEE ■

The county seat of Alfalfa County, Cherokee is home to farms that are largely family owned and operated.

Longhorn, AMES
This spotted longhorn is a common sight at Island Guest Ranch—a working dude ranch that offers visitors a chance to take part in the action.

■ Turner Falls, DAVIS

■ **Sunrise, MAYSVILLE**

Daybreak meets mist on this summer day in Maysville—once home to pilot Wiley Post.

I have traveled the state from corner to corner, and our topography encompasses the best of America's landscape. As First Lady, I have gotten to know Oklahomans firsthand, and we have a pioneer spirit that transcends time. We truly put the "heart" in heartland.

— **CATHY KEATING**
First Lady of Oklahoma, 1995-2003

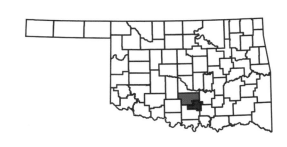

Foggy Morning, KENTON ◼
On this morning, earth and air of differing temperatures
make for a natural halo at Black Mesa State Park.

◼ **Red Hill, POND CREEK**
The mesas rise from the surrounding prairie near Pond Creek in Grant County,
unveiling "Chief Wakita," the silhouette of a Native American on horseback.

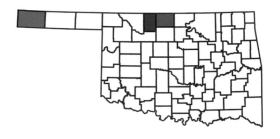

■ **Great Salt Plains of Oklahoma, ALFALFA COUNTY**

This aerial photo shows the vast expanse of the Great Salt Plains of Oklahoma in Alfalfa County in north-central Oklahoma. The Salt Plains were formed over millions of years by repeated flooding of seawater that became trapped in the area. The water evaporated, leaving salt deposits. This was a rich source of salt for the indigenous tribes and early pioneers who first settled the area. A wildlife refuge was established here in 1930, and has become an important feeding and resting area for migratory waterfowl and endangered species.

DID YOU KNOW?	The Tallgrass Prairie Preserve in northern Oklahoma is the largest protected remnant of tallgrass prairie left on earth.

■ Arkansas River, near COWLINGTON

Oklahoma operates several ports that lead directly to the Gulf of Mexico. A major tributary of the Mississippi River and the fourth-longest river in the nation, the Arkansas River connects ports in Muskogee and Catoosa.

■ **Evening Star and Quarter Moon, ATOKA**

Grassland, Red Slough Wildlife Management Area, IDABEL ■

A 5,814-acre wetland, the Red Slough Wildlife Management Area is known throughout the region as a premier bird-watching and waterfowl-hunting area. It is a very popular southeastern Oklahoma recreational destination.

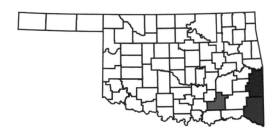

Pampas Grass, JET ■

Morning light shines through the pampas grass at Great Salt Plains State Park. The park sits next to Salt Plains National Wildlife Refuge—one of the few places on the earth where visitors can dig for hourglass selenite crystals.

Palisades, Cimarron River, FREEDOM (right) ■

■ **Thunderhead, WAGONER**
A massive thunderhead cloud takes shape in a storm over Wagoner.

■ Plowed Abstract, BESSIE
From the sky, these rows of plowed field
in Bessie are just stripes on the earth.

Our old Indian Territory homeland was first populated by Indians of various tribes—the most generous, greed-free cultures on our planet. Then came the Sooners, drawn in by their yen for land, freedom and open space. The territory offered none of the gold and silver dreams that lured others to California. Take that population base, add the fact that geography separates us from the East Coast centers of wealth and high culture, and one can understand why Oklahoma friendships are formed of something besides financial status or college degrees. And why, when my pickup breaks down on an Oklahoma road, I know the first vehicle to come along will stop to offer help. We know we are all just people, and it shows.

— TONY HILLERMAN
Decorated WWII veteran and author

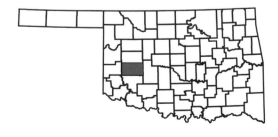

■ Grand Lake O' the Cherokees, GROVE

DID YOU KNOW? Oklahoma contains more miles of shoreline than the Atlantic and Gulf Coasts combined.

ARTS

Arts—A Wonderful, Surprising Mosaic

Drive down Highway 283 just north of Altus, and soon you will see an abandoned garage. At first glance, it looks like nothing more than a building long past its prime. But if you stop and look closer, you'll discover a bright tile mosaic carefully constructed on one of the garage's exterior walls.

That colorful mosaic includes both large pieces and small shards of tile, artfully arranged in sunbursts and swirls. The larger pieces anchor and define the mosaic. It's the smaller shards, however, that add detail and complexity, and turn the collection of tile remnants into something beautiful.

Oklahoma's Arts scene is just as surprising as that mosaic—more robust and colorful than anyone could ever imagine. Oklahoma boasts large, well-established performance powerhouses and institutions that anchor the state's cultural offerings. But smaller—and equally talented—independent artists, musicians and cultural contributions are just as important.

Like the mosaic, Oklahoma's Arts join both large and small pieces to form a beautifully complete picture.

One can't imagine the Arts in Oklahoma without immediately thinking of the "big pieces" of our cultural mosaic. Both Oklahoma City and Tulsa—as well as other smaller cities—are home to internationally recognized performance groups.

The Tulsa Ballet, for example, is consistently ranked one of the top 10 ballet companies in the country. And Oklahoma City's Ballet Oklahoma is renowned for performing an eclectic mix of traditional and new ballets.

Equally impressive is Tulsa Opera, Oklahoma's professional opera company. As one of the oldest opera companies in North America (founded in 1948), Tulsa Opera presents both familiar works and company premieres, and consistently ranks among the best regional opera companies in the United States.

No discussion of major cultural players would be complete without the state's symphony orchestras. Tulsa, Bartlesville and Enid all

1 Garage Mosaic, ALTUS

2 OK Mozart Outdoor Concert, Woolaroc, BARTLESVILLE

are home to widely respected symphonies. And the Oklahoma City Philharmonic, founded in 1938, performs in the acoustically outstanding Civic Center Music Hall. Early in its history, the orchestra gained international acclaim from a regular series of radio broadcasts to American troops abroad. Now, the Philharmonic presents both classics and pops concerts each season, ensuring Oklahomans will always have a place to experience world-class orchestral music.

Oklahoma City is also home to one of the premier art museums in the region, the Oklahoma City Museum of Art. It contains the most comprehensive collection of Dale Chihuly Glass in the world, including

a 55-foot tower comprised of 2,100 hand-blown glass parts. The museum is also a local hot spot, with its Roof Terrace offering warm-weather Thursday-night "Cocktails on the Skyline" to those who gather for socializing and admiring the downtown cityscape.

Tulsa's Gilcrease Museum is one of the country's greatest institutions for the preservation and study of American art and history. Located in the Osage hills just northwest of downtown Tulsa, this "Museum of the Americas" is the product of a lifetime of collecting by oilman Thomas Gilcrease.

A surprise gift to Tulsa by oilman Waite Phillips and his wife, Genevieve, Philbrook Museum of Art is housed in the Phillips' 1927 Italianate villa in one of the city's most beautiful neighborhoods. It is one of only five U.S. museums that combine a historic home, gardens and collections. After enjoying the collections inside, visitors can step outside to stroll the immaculate gardens—including dramatic sculptures, inviting paths and a children's maze and sensory garden.

The Fred Jones Jr. Museum of Art at the University of Oklahoma, home to an 8,000-object permanent collection, is another jewel in Oklahoma's crown. Recognized as one of the finest university art museums in the United States, its newly expanded facility is an architectural triumph that would be at home in any major city.

1 Air Force Monument, Couch Park, OKLAHOMA CITY

3 Mural, ALVA

2 "Oklahoma Centennial Land Run Monument," OKLAHOMA CITY

Future artists also have a home at the Oklahoma Arts Institute, the state's official school of the arts, located in the pristine Quartz Mountain State Park in Lone Wolf. Each year, the Institute hosts its Summer Arts Institute, which provides unparalleled arts education for high-school students.

For a decidedly Oklahoman twist on the traditional Arts scene, the National Cowboy & Western Heritage Museum in Oklahoma City provides a window into the state's past. In addition to showcasing one of the finest collections of Western art in the nation, the museum contains a 14,000-square-foot, circa-1900 Western cattle town. It also is home to the American Cowboy Gallery, an extensive exhibition about the working cowboy in the United States.

But even as these big players anchor Oklahoma's Arts scene, local and independent artists and organizations help bring our state's "mosaic" into focus. Almost every small community seems to have a playhouse or theater that provides high-quality theatrical and musical events. And independent artists continue Oklahoma's pioneer spirit by showcasing their unique perspectives in local galleries and at art shows.

Unique to Oklahoma's Art mosaic is the Native American tribes' cultural centers. The Cherokee Heritage Center, located in the foothills of the Ozark Mountains, is but one example of the rich Native

1 "Crossing the Red," ALTUS

2 First United Methodist Church, MANGUM

American culture that continues to thrive today. Here, the Tsa-La-Gi Ancient Village is a living museum that re-creates the way a traditional Cherokee community lived prior to European contact. Visitors can witness villagers going about their daily routines, preparing meals, playing ancient games like stickball, and participating in arts like basket weaving and flint knapping.

Contemporary intertribal powwows, held throughout the state, allow Native Americans to share their culture, art and music. Tribes come together for singing, dancing, feasting, selling, trading arts and crafts, and upholding traditional customs.

Oklahoma is also home to a rich collection of public art. Statues, sculptures, gardens and murals are found not only in the large metro areas, but also in small towns throughout the state.

While the state's Art mosaic includes both big and small pieces, it needs a strong "glue" to hold the pieces together. The glue in Oklahoma is music—with a rich heritage that crosses many genres and, for decades, has united the state.

Oklahoma may be best known for its country music artists, such as Garth Brooks, Ronnie Brooks (of Brooks & Dunn), Roy Clark, Vince Gill, Woody Guthrie, Toby Keith, Reba McEntire and Carrie Underwood. But country is only a part of our musical story.

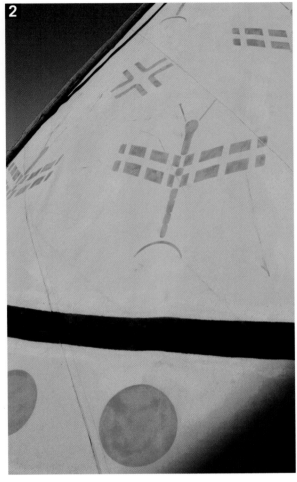

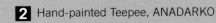
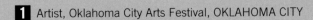

1 Artist, Oklahoma City Arts Festival, OKLAHOMA CITY

2 Hand-painted Teepee, ANADARKO

Western or "cowboy" music began prior to Oklahoma's settlement, created by cowboys whose traditional singing style became a well-recognized, romantic ideal as the cowboy grew in America's cultural imagination.

Oklahoma played a big role in the creation of Western Swing, a fusion of country music, jazz, pop and blues aimed at dancers. Bob Wills and His Texas Playboys were based in Tulsa at the still-popular Cain's Ballroom, known for its spring-loaded dance floor.

Although many of today's top country music artists hail from Oklahoma, steel guitar and banjo aren't all we play here. Oklahoma has a rich jazz, blues and gospel heritage. The Oklahoma Jazz Hall of Fame recognizes this history and strives to "create unity through music." Each June, as part of the annual Juneteenth observance, the Hall of Fame inducts a new class of Oklahoma musicians who have made important contributions to the musical landscape.

Native sons and daughters from all musical genres have gone on to find huge success. Composer Jimmy Webb, a native of Elk City, is one of the most honored songwriters of our time. David Gates, founder of the

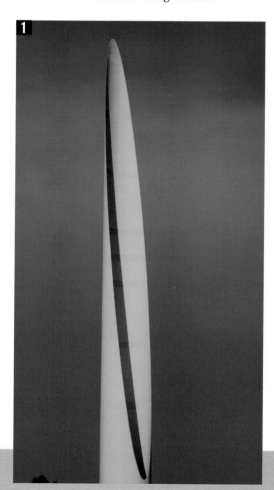

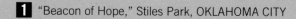
1 "Beacon of Hope," Stiles Park, OKLAHOMA CITY

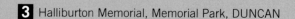
3 Halliburton Memorial, Memorial Park, DUNCAN

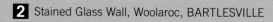
2 Stained Glass Wall, Woolaroc, BARTLESVILLE

1970's super-group Bread, also called Oklahoma home. And one can't forget greats like, Gene Autry, J.J. Cale, Kristin Chenoweth, Patti Page, Leon Russell and The Flaming Lips, just to name a few.

But while we know how to swing and rock, Oklahomans also appreciate and embrace classical music. Bartlesville's internationally acclaimed OK Mozart festival draws approximately 20,000 visitors each year and culminates in an outdoor concert held at historic Woolaroc, the former country home of oilman Frank Phillips that is now a 3,600-acre ranch and wildlife preserve.

Oklahoma's Art mosaic is unexpected. It runs the gamut from local artists with unique approaches to well-known performance groups to Native American dancing and crafts. This mix of Arts—and appreciation of things both familiar and completely new—is quintessentially Oklahoman.

You'll find art everywhere in Oklahoma. Just turn the corner and keep your eyes—and ears—open.

1 Discoveryland, TULSA

2 Mural, ANADARKO

Shattuck Windmill Museum, SHATTUCK ■
The Shattuck Windmill Museum and Park contains 45 vintage windmills and one wind generator. The museum stands as a reminder of Oklahoma's prairie past, when the nearest stream or lake could be miles away and pumping water out of the ground was necessary for survival.

■ **Enid Symphony Center, ENID**

The audience is captivated as Grammy-winning lyric-spinto soprano (and Enid native) Leona Mitchell performs in this exquisitely decorated hall, where fine acoustics were paramount in every detail during the center's recent renovation—including the painted royal carpet.

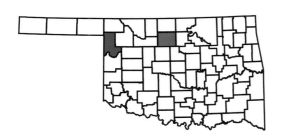

A s a young girl growing up in Oklahoma, I was convinced that any dream I had was possible. Two amazing Oklahomans, Maurine Morrow Priebe and Inez Silberg, helped me focus and nurture my dream. And now it is time for all of us to be about the business of encouraging the precious dreams of our youth.

— **LEONA MITCHELL**
Internationally acclaimed lyric-spinto soprano

■ **Bronze Longhorn, Stockyards City, OKLAHOMA CITY**
This steer's head greets visitors from its position above the main entrance.
Stockyards City is the largest stocker/feeder cattle market in the world.

> "**H**ome Sweet Oklahoma" is how I've always felt about my state. My heart is filled with pride, love and beautiful memories.
>
> — **PATTI PAGE**
> *Platinum-selling recording artist*

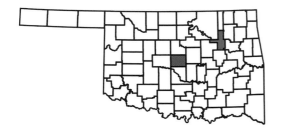

Oklahoma's All-Star Centennial Band, OKLAHOMA CITY ■
Composed of the finest marching band students from high schools throughout the state, this band represented Oklahoma by leading the Rose Parade in the 2007 Pasadena Tournament of Roses.

Philbrook Museum of Art, TULSA ■

Built in 1927 by oilman Waite Phillips, Philbrook has evolved from a family
estate to a nationally known art center. Following a recent renovation, the
gardens at Philbrook provide as much beauty outside as the art does inside.

▪ Silhouettes, ENID

At Government Springs Park, one may look twice before realizing this cattle-drive scene is only a clever silhouette. A tribute to the cattle drovers who traveled that very land when it was the Chisholm Trail, the complete scene includes cattle, cowboys, a chuck wagon and a single Native American.

■ Dick Tracy Mural, PAWNEE

Gripping audiences in both American and international newspapers for 46 years, this yellow-jacketed legend sprung from the mind of cartoonist and Pawnee native Chester Gould. This commemorative mural is the largest Dick Tracy cartoon in the world.

Oklahoma International Bluegrass Festival, GUTHRIE ■

This three-day festival held every October draws more than 15,000 bluegrass enthusiasts. Since 1996, musicians from all over the world have taken the stage, including Vince Gill and the Sam Bush Band. In addition to the performances, the festival supports musical arts education through music scholarships and other educational opportunities.

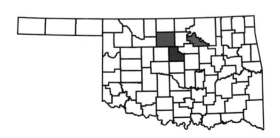

■ Fred Jones Jr. Museum of Art, NORMAN (left)

Shown is the Mary and Howard Lester Wing, which houses the Weitzenhoffer Collection, an astounding personal collection of French Impressionism presented in replica rooms as they were originally displayed during private ownership. The architecturally minimalist museum, owned by the University of Oklahoma, emphasizes the importance of both the artwork and its creators.

DID YOU KNOW?	The 50,000-square-foot Sam Noble Oklahoma Museum of Natural History is the largest university-based museum in the United States.

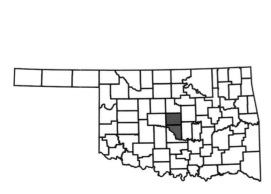

Beadwork, Red Earth Festival, OKLAHOMA CITY ■

Paseo Arts District Mural, OKLAHOMA CITY

This fountain mural welcomes visitors to the historic Paseo Arts District. The area, which dates back to 1929, became an environment for artists to share and exchange ideas in the 1970s. It is now home to eateries, shops, and more than 60 artists and 17 galleries dedicated to photography, glass blowing, wood carving, sculpture, painting, sketching and an ever-changing emergence of progressive art forms.

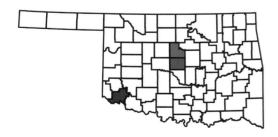

Vintage Coca-Cola Mural, GUTHRIE ■

■ **"Vision Seeker," ALTUS**

Harold T. Holden unveiled this life-size bronze statue of a warrior chief in 1996.

Depot Mural, ALVA ■
This is one of several large wall murals that bring history to life.
It depicts a day in the life of travelers at the old Alva Depot.

■ **Will Rogers Memorial Museum, CLAREMORE**

> **I** am proud to be an Osage and to have been born in Oklahoma! I remember very well going to the Indian dances. We still attend the Grayhorse dances in June!
>
> — **MARIA TALLCHIEF**
> *Former New York City Ballet prima ballerina and founder of the Chicago City Ballet*

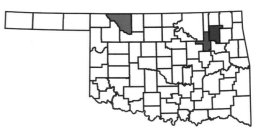

■ **"Swan Lake," Performing Arts Center, TULSA (left)**
Professional ballerinas of the Tulsa Ballet grace the stage to the music of Tchaikovsky.

■ Buffalo Sculpture, MEDICINE PARK

This unusual metal buffalo was created by sculptor Robert E. Dean. Pieces by this Waurika native are largely natural and often inspired by Native American ideas. Dean credits his use of wire welding, as in this piece, to his artistic influence, Dareld Swinford.

Growing up in Oklahoma, I remember watching tumbleweeds roll across the prairie, envious that they were on a journey, yearning for my own journey to begin. At night, I would lie in the grass and gaze up at the vast Oklahoma sky, knowing with all the certainty of childhood that, one day, my journey would take me to those very stars, and I would gaze back on my home from space.

— SHANNON LUCID
NASA astronaut

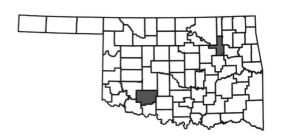

Cain's Ballroom, TULSA ■

Cain's Ballroom was built in the heart of an oil-boom city in 1924. Originally intended as a garage for one of the city's founders, Tate Brady (as in the Brady Arts District and Brady Theater), it quickly transformed into a popular nightspot. In 1930, Madison W. "Daddy" Cain bought the building and named it Cain's Dance Academy. People from all over came to hear that "hot hillbilly music," which came to be known as Western Swing, played by one of the most popular bands of the day, Bob Wills and His Texas Playboys. Today, with its famous spring-loaded dance floor, Cain's Ballroom showcases music of all genres, from Oklahoma-grown The Flaming Lips to country legend Willie Nelson.

■ Leon Russell Star, Cain's Ballroom, TULSA

The sidewalk outside of Cain's Ballroom is lined with stars of famous performers who have played the historic venue. In addition to Leon Russell, stars like Roy Clark, Merle Haggard, Hank Williams, Jr., and Arlo Guthrie point to the Cain's as a special place to entertain.

■ Standing Bear Statue, PONCA CITY

Oreland C. Joe's 22-foot bronze depiction of Ponca Chief Standing Bear pays tribute to the chieftain's 19th century contributions to the advancement of Native American civil rights. Located in 63-acre Standing Bear Native American Memorial Park, the statue is centered in a large viewing court, complete with six decorative tribal seals and eight Ponca Tribe clan name inlays.

> **A**t the Capitol in Washington, D.C., stands a statue of Will Rogers facing the legislature so that, "he could keep an eye on Congress!" Oklahomans are like that—very conscientious, honorable and good humored. It's what I love most about Oklahoma—the people!
>
> — **STEVE LARGENT**
> *NFL Hall of Fame wide receiver*

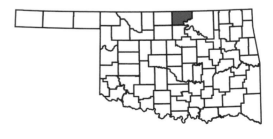

Fairgrounds Pavilion, TULSA ■

Designed by Leland I. Shumway and built in 1932, the pavilion has eight separate entrances, each with decorative depictions of horses, steers and rams in terra cotta detail.

Cowboy Tack, GUTHRIE (right) ■

■ **"Giants of the Great Plains," GRANITE**

This mosaic monument in pink granite honors the life and legacy of Will Rogers, the highly regarded humorist, actor and social commentator.

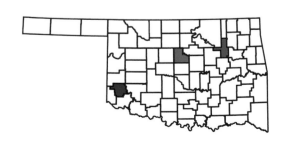

■ OKLAHOMA CITY MUSEUM OF ART, OKLAHOMA CITY

Among the many fine exhibits in the Oklahoma City Museum of Art is the world's most comprehensive Dale Chihuly glass collection, with pieces spanning three decades. The museum is also home to the artist's tallest piece of instillation art, the "Eleanor Blake Kirkpatrick Memorial Tower." Chihuly is praised for his interdisciplinary techniques and masterful use of natural light, which invite the eye through colorful layers of translucent and transparent glass. Of 200 impressive Chihuly museum collections across the world, the state of Oklahoma boasts two, the other at the Fine Arts Institute of Edmond.

> **B**eing from Oklahoma means that every time you come back, your family is waiting for you. The entire state is your family and they graciously welcome you home. There's nowhere like Oklahoma.
>
> — JENNIFER BERRY
> *Miss America 2006*

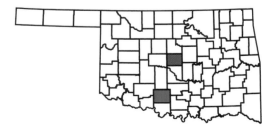

■ "On the Chisholm Trail," DUNCAN

Commissioned by the McCasland Foundation to honor the cowboys and pioneers who settled Stephens County, "On the Chisholm Trail" by Oklahoma artist Paul Moore stands 11 feet high and stretches nearly 35 feet across the horizon. The sculptor is also creating an enormous bronze rendering of the Land Run of 1889, titled "Oklahoma Centennial Land Run Monument." Consisting of 38 people, 34 horses and three wagons, among many other elements, the final sculpture will extend more than 100 yards, making it one of the world's largest bronze works.

DID YOU KNOW?   The world's most extensive collection of celebrated glass-sculptor Dale Chihuly's work is at the Oklahoma City Museum of Art.

"Gates of Time," Oklahoma City National Memorial, OKLAHOMA CITY ■
This is one of two gates that stand at each end of the memorial, connected by a reflecting pool. The gates are marked with "9:01" and "9:03"—the instants surrounding the 9:02 a.m. bombing. The events of that cruel day revealed the strength of our people, as Oklahomans stood together with resolve and compassion.

■ **"And Jesus Wept," Oklahoma City National Memorial, OKLAHOMA CITY**
St. Joseph's Catholic Church narrowly survived the 1995 blast. In memory of those lost, the church erected this statue near the memorial site. An unofficial element of the memorial, the piece is widely appreciated by visitors.

Our state is a place where an enterprising and courageous people built cities and careers, and responded as one when confronted with the unexpected or the unspeakable. Oklahomans are an extraordinary people.

— **FRANK KEATING**
Governor of Oklahoma, 1995-2003

■ "The Chairs," Oklahoma City National Memorial, OKLAHOMA CITY

These chairs, designed by Hans and Torrey Butzer and Sven Berg, stand in remembrance of the 168 people who lost their lives on April 19, 1995, when the Alfred P. Murrah Federal Building was the site of a tragic act of domestic terrorism. The 19 children who died are represented by smaller chairs. Each chair is constructed of stone, bronze and glass, and carries the name of the victim it represents.

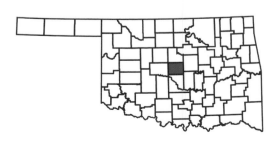

■ "Seed Sower," NORMAN

This 12-foot bronze monument has become an icon for the University of Oklahoma. The first statue was cast in 2000 by sculptor Paul Moore and was placed in the South Oval of the university's main campus in Norman. The two years following saw "Seed Sower" castings bloom at the University of Oklahoma Health Sciences Centers in Tulsa and Oklahoma City.

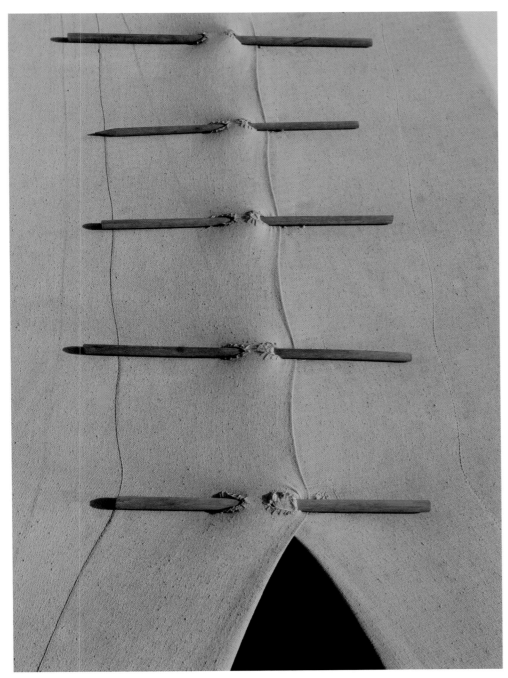

■ **Teepee Detail, ANADARKO**

Lobby Ceiling, TULSA ■
This intricate mosaic invites all eyes upward
in the lobby of the 320 S. Boston Building.

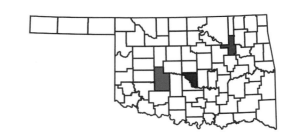

Stained Glass Wall, First Presbyterian Church, BARTLESVILLE (right) ■

■ Fiddles, GUTHRIE

While often handled with Oklahoma bluegrass charm, this instrument also plays a major note in the state's rich orchestral offerings. Enid is home of Oklahoma's earliest orchestra. Unmatched cultural events, such as Bartlesville's annual OK Mozart festival, draw internationally renowned talent to the state. Oklahoma encourages youth to cultivate their musical skill through impressive venues like the Oklahoma Arts Institute at breathtaking Quartz Mountain. So influential is the program that in 1983, it was expanded to include expert instruction for adults as well.

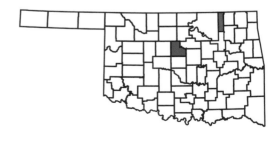

■ Native American Boots, Red Earth Festival, OKLAHOMA CITY

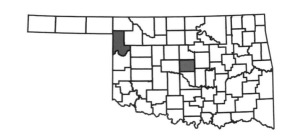

■ Ranch Gate Detail, HARMON (left)

Iron Gazebo, Gilcrease Museum, TULSA ■

■ "Land of Hope," NEWKIRK
Figurative sculptor Bernadette Hess Carman illustrates emotions
artistically. In this frozen moment, she vividly captures the hope
a pioneer couple exudes as they embark on a new land.

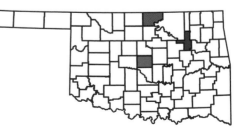

■ Dome Ceiling, Oklahoma State Capitol, **OKLAHOMA CITY**

Dreamcatchers, PONCA CITY ■
Native American legend holds that these handmade items "trap" bad dreams and provide a restful night's sleep when positioned over the bed. These dreamcatchers are part of the Native American crafts featured at a powwow at Standing Bear Native American Memorial Park.

■ **DeSteiguer Building, GUTHRIE**

■ **Cherokee Trading Post, WEATHERFORD (left)**

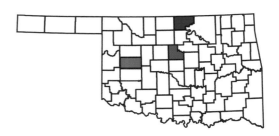

■ American Flag Mural, WATONGA

> **G**rowing up in Oklahoma helped instill in me the kind of values and work ethic that allowed me to be successful not only in basketball but in life. Those same values are being passed on to my children, and I can pass them on with confidence because I know they work.
>
> — MARK PRICE
> *Four-time NBA All-Star*

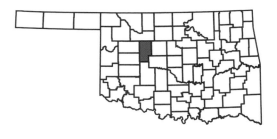

Price Tower, BARTLESVILLE ■

World-famous architect Frank Lloyd Wright built the Price Tower in 1956. At 19 stories, this National Historic Landmark is Wright's tallest project and only skyscraper. Originally conceived for New York City, Wright called the design "the tree that escaped the crowded forest." The building today houses art exhibits, an exceptional hotel, fine dining and exclusive shopping.

■ Prayer Tower, Oral Roberts University, TULSA

Highly symbolic architecture complements the meticulously maintained Prayer Garden in the center of campus. This 200-foot tower resembles a cross and signifies the relationship between man and God.

Chickasaw Nation Capitol, TISHOMINGO ■

This 1898 granite Victorian Gothic structure was repurchased by the Chickasaw Nation in 1989 after it served as the Johnston County Courthouse.

■ The Gray Bros. Building, GUTHRIE

This decorative turret is an example of the historic commercial architecture that characterizes Oklahoma's first state capital. Guthrie is the nation's largest Historic District, as designated by the United States' Department of the Interior.

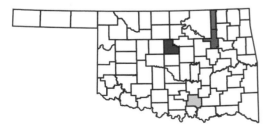

Boston Avenue United Methodist Church, TULSA ■

With her unique vision for Boston Avenue United Methodist Church, Dr. Adah Robinson, a University of Tulsa art instructor, was chosen in the 1920s to design this Art Deco gem. The building includes a 15-story tower (elevator-equipped since 1963) and a round sanctuary. The stunning interior is decorated with beautiful stained glass windows and Art Deco mosaics.

■ **Kachina Doll, ELK CITY**

This ornamental Kachina doll is one of two that welcomes visitors to the National Route 66 Museum,

part of the Old Town Museum Complex, which is home to numerous museums and historic attractions.

I've had the good fortune to travel the world. I could have chosen anywhere to settle, but I always came home to Oklahoma. I have always taken solace in knowing that Oklahoma was mine to return to.

— **GAILARD SARTAIN**
Actor, comedian, artist and writer

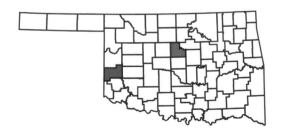

BUSINESS AND TECHNOLOGY

A State of Possibilities

As Oklahoma enters its second century, the future is as rich with possibilities as it was at the time of the state's founding. Lured by the promise of land and a chance for prosperity, early Oklahomans carried hopes, dreams and a vision for the future across the sweeping plains of Indian Territory. Today, that same Sooner vision and hope are alive and well—in Oklahoma enterprises large and small.

From the beginning, Oklahomans have demonstrated a knack for recognizing opportunity and realizing potential. Even

statehood itself was little more than a possibility until a group of founders made that dream a reality. Statehood signaled the start of an era in which "what if" had every possibility of becoming "what is." And there's been no stopping us since. Now, as then, extraordinary opportunities exist for Oklahoma to capture the spotlight and make an impact on both a national and global scale.

Around here, the glass is always half full. Known for our can-do attitude and hands-on style, Oklahomans take special pride in the ability to imagine and shape the future. It's no surprise, then, that many of the state's economic milestones are rooted in a willingness to entertain possibilities. Through sheer determination, the dreams of ordinary men and women became

groundbreaking discoveries, many of which put tiny Oklahoma towns on the map.

Such was the case when a group of wildcatters experimented with nitroglycerin to open Chelsea's Nellie Johnstone No. 1 in 1897, tapping the vast Mid-Continent Reservoir stretching from central Texas to eastern Kansas. The state's first commercial well soon had company when a gusher in the Glenn Pool ignited an oil boom the likes of which may never come again. It was the world's richest field to date, producing more than 120,000 barrels daily, and generating more money than the California Gold Rush and Colorado Silver Rush combined.

1 American Airlines Maintenance Facility, TULSA

3 Field's Pies, PAULS VALLEY

2 Ruby's Melons, RUSH SPRINGS

Turning innovation into enterprise has become a hallmark of Oklahoma business. Many of the state's early entrepreneurs achieved great success in their day while laying the groundwork for innovation and accomplishments yet to come. People like the Williams brothers, who turned a sidewalk construction business into a renowned energy company with a nationwide network of oil pipelines. Now, many of those pipelines, long since decommissioned, comprise a fiber-optic network that serves advertising, sports, news and entertainment companies worldwide. Recasting those oil pipelines helped launch the modern telecommunications industry.

In recent years, opportunities for launching new businesses in Oklahoma have extended to more than just a lucky few. Entrepreneurship has become an important career option that will determine the state's future economy. Oklahoma's long tradition of encouraging and rewarding risk-takers endures today, thanks in part to strategic alliances both public and private. Across the state, business and industry are partnering with government agencies, technical schools, colleges and universities to provide the very best educational opportunities, training and internships.

Leading the way is the Oklahoma Department of Career and Technology Education's expansive vocational-technical network. Recognized as one of the nation's two most outstanding workforce

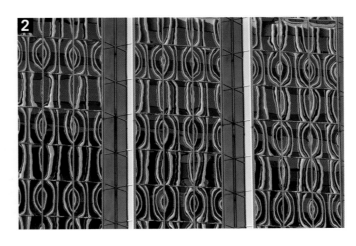

training programs, Oklahoma's CareerTech spans 56 campuses, 398 school districts, 25 correctional skill centers and three juvenile facilities. The system's Learning Network has opened a world of possibilities and educational options for Oklahomans with around-the-clock access to Web-based and interactive

1 Mister Pat Barge, FORT COFFEE

3 Dream Valley Farm, LAWTON

2 Leadership Square, OKLAHOMA CITY

BUSINESS AND TECHNOLOGY

training from home, work and the classroom. One of the most valuable weapons in the state's arsenal of economic incentives is CareerTech's Training for Industry Program (TIP), which develops start-up training programs for new and expanding industries.

Recruiting Oklahoma's best and brightest through economic diversification and job creation is a statewide goal. While communities do their share to foster business-friendly climates, state agencies, trade associations, foundations and organizations of every stripe are pooling resources to seed new endeavors and support start-up businesses. One such initiative is the Oklahoma Center for the Advancement of Science and Technology (OCAST). Dozens of budding entrepreneurs have obtained make-or-break financing through this state-funded program, recognized nationally and internationally as a model of best practices.

Turning high-tech innovations into actual business opportunities is the job of the Oklahoma Technology Commercialization Center (OTCC). Hundreds of companies have benefitted from OTCC's assistance, many focusing on groundbreaking medical and nanotechnology research. Manipulating materials on a molecular level, researchers are using nanotechnology to make ordinary products extraordinary. Already consumers can buy stain-repelling, wrinkle-free pants, and tennis rackets that are twice as strong and twice as stable as before and

1 Koch Fertilizer Plant, ENID

2 Hay Bales, BURLINGTON

incredibly lightweight. In years to come, nanomaterials are thought to have the potential to help people overcome paralysis and even blindness.

As one of the first six states to develop a nanotechnology initiative, Oklahoma is again at the forefront of emerging industries, with five Oklahoma universities adding nanotechnology classes. Together, these efforts are bringing more high-performance, high-tech firms, higher per capita income, and improved quality of life for all Oklahomans.

Once thought of largely as wheat and cattle country, Oklahoma agriculture is also expanding to meet 21st century demands and economic realities. Today, few North American

crops aren't grown in Oklahoma. Poultry and pigs, for example, now rank second and third among the state's agricultural industries. Other top crops include corn, pecans, soybeans and peanuts. And, contrary to Oklahoma's association with the Plains States, more than 6 million acres of commercial timber production contribute more than $1.5 billion to our economy each year.

Despite our agricultural advances, Oklahomans are never far from the sources of the state's bounty. A growing number of community farmers markets and co-ops allow consumers to meet the folks who grow their food face to face. "Agritourism" is another largely untapped revenue source that

landowners are just beginning to explore. More and more urbanites are finding authentic rural experiences down on Oklahoma's farms and ranches. Some come to hunt and fish, others to cut their own Christmas trees, pick berries or simply purchase a jar of local jam. Previously limited opportunities to explore rural traditions and lifestyles and enjoy nature's bounty are expanding to meet ever-growing demand. Working ranches, dairy and vegetable farms, berry patches, and tree farms all are enjoying renewed interest and bursts of business.

1 Train Engine, ANADARKO

3 Grape Ranch Vineyards, OKEMAH

2 Pump Jack, POND CREEK

One of the most promising agritourism endeavors may be Oklahoma's burgeoning wine industry. Acreages once dotted with oil pumpers are being planted with vines as viticulture, the science of grape growing, takes root. This second grape boom—the first was cut short by Prohibition—is gathering momentum as local vineyards become popular weekend destinations. Some 38 licensed wineries draw hundreds of visitors each year to tasting rooms and harvest festivals complete with grape stomping.

As a virtual "crossroads of America," Oklahoma is uniquely positioned, perhaps even destined, to become a hub for aviation and aerospace industries. Nearly 300 aerospace companies now operating in the state could soon propel the region to one of the top aircraft maintenance, repair and overhaul markets in the world.

Oklahoma can lay claim to a host of aviation achievements and pioneers. Record-setters Will Rogers and Wiley Post come to mind, but also pilot Charles Willard, who circled Oklahoma City at 75 feet

in the state's first airplane in 1910, and Clyde Cessna, who flight-tested his first plane a year later. In the decade that followed, Curtiss-Wright Corporation, the world's largest

airplane manufacturer, was persuaded by Oklahoma's "air-minded attitude" to land in the state capital. Then, in 1928, Tom Braniff initiated the first commercial passenger flight between Oklahoma City and Tulsa, while oilman Erle Halliburton established Southwest Air Fast Express, later known as American Airlines—a company that maintains its Oklahoma ties to this day, most notably through its mammoth aircraft maintenance facility housed at the Tulsa International Airport.

Oklahoma's growing aviation industry was further fueled by the U.S. military. Vance Air Force Base was an important pilot training facility during World War II, and

1 Devon Energy Building, OKLAHOMA CITY

2 Tractor in Field, MANCHESTER

now trains Navy and Marine Corps aviators. Tinker Air Force Base is a major military installation and the state's largest single-site employer. Altus Air Force Base has become the Air Force's premier air mobility training center.

In the years to come, you might well see more than hawks making lazy circles in the sky. As the state that has produced more astronauts than any other, it's only fitting that Oklahoma figures prominently in the pursuit of space tourism. Burns Flat in Washita County is the site of the country's only inland spaceport. With 13,000 feet of runway, the former Clinton-Sherman Air Force Base is set to become a landing site for the world's first commercial

space flights. Rocketplane, Inc., an Oklahoma company, is developing a reusable launching vehicle to maintain the International Space Station and envisions commercial passenger space flights in just a few short years.

If all Oklahoma businesses share fundamental principles, tenacity and hard work certainly are two of the most important. In fact, you might say that hard work is one of our core beliefs. It is the state motto after all. *Labor omnia vincit*—labor conquers all things. And in many ways, it has. Thanks to those early visionaries and so many others who followed, Oklahoma has emerged as an economic powerhouse firmly anchored by a distinctive and colorful past.

Oklahomans will continue to look to the future and reach for the stars. And to build on the successes of the men and women who saw the possibilities in what was, who had the imagination to dream what could be and who possessed the commitment to see it through.

 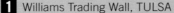

1 Williams Trading Wall, TULSA

2 Maize Barn, P_Bar Farms, WEATHERFORD

 3 Bass Pro Shop, OKLAHOMA CITY

Pump Jack Silhouette, EDMOND ■

Dell Call Center, OKLAHOMA CITY ■

Dell's Customer Contact Center opened in 2005 and employs more than 1,000 Oklahomans who provide sales and technical assistance to Dell customers from all over North America.

■ **Tinker Air Force Base, MIDWEST CITY**

This E-3 Sentry is a military airborne warning and control system (AWACS) aircraft based at Tinker. The AWACS aircraft provide all-weather surveillance, command, control and communications to the United States, NATO and other air-defense forces.

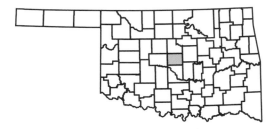

■ Pete's Place, KREBS

Looking for a way to support his family after suffering a mining injury, Pete Prichard began making and serving homemade Choc beer to area miners. Soon, he found himself also fixing lunches for these men in his home kitchen. The workers liked the food over at "Pete's Place" and the word quickly spread. Pete officially opened Pete's Place restaurant in his home in 1925. Gradually, Pete expanded his menu and added homemade wine. Today, the third generation of Prichards serves authentic Italian cuisine in that same location—although the family no longer lives upstairs.

I enjoy reminiscing over photographs and recalling childhood memories. Many of these photos are of places I have seen and enjoyed, and that have had a huge impact on my life.

— JAMES GARNER

Oscar-nominated and Emmy Award-winning television and film actor

World's Largest McDonald's, VINITA ■
The Golden Arches stretch over Interstate 44, east of Tulsa, near Vinita. This McDonald's, billed as the world's largest (in square footage), has been serving hamburgers and fries to hungry travelers since 1975.

■ Cattle Drive, VICI

Oklahoma ranchers house an inventory of about 5.1 million
head of cattle annually worth approximately $3.7 billion.

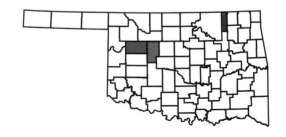

■ **Watonga Cheese Plant, WATONGA**

These metal containers shape many different types of cheeses.
Since 1940, Watonga Cheese Plant has supplied specialties
like Oklahoma-shaped cheeses to dairy lovers everywhere.

ConocoPhillips Tower, BARTLESVILLE ■

> I loved growing up in Tulsa. In the summer, we
> rode our bikes everywhere, swam all day at the
> neighborhood pool, and after dinner played softball
> in the front yard with the Mimosa tree as first base
> and the gas meter as second. We all knew our
> neighbors and everyone looked out for each other.
>
> — MARY KAY PLACE
> *Emmy award-winning actress*

Mechanized Irrigation, TYRONE ■

This technology has allowed the panhandle to transform from

■ Peanuts, MADILL

South-central Oklahoma's own Clint Williams Company is one of the
few remaining family-run peanut distributors, supplying the nation
and the world with peanut products, specialties and gift baskets.

Ear of Corn, NOWATA COUNTY ■

■ Farmers Market, WAPANUCKA

Fresh potatoes and tomatoes are on the menu at this farmers market
in the southern Oklahoma county of Johnston.

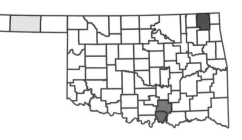

United States Postal Service National Center for Employee Development, NORMAN ■

This giant 72-acre USPS site contains training, meeting and housing facilities, which total nearly 740,000 square feet. The center conducts more than just postal training. Professionals from a variety of fields learn job skills in these plush surroundings, which include an Olympic-size pool, whirlpool and sauna, fully staffed fitness center, and two cafeterias.

■ OG&E Plant, Sooner Lake, RED ROCK (left)

OG&E's Sooner Power Plant in northern Oklahoma uses the most efficient proven technology for coal-fired electric generation. In total, OG&E serves nearly 800,000 customers in a service area that spans 30,000 square miles in Oklahoma and western Arkansas. The company generates electricity from eight power plants and two wind farms.

DID YOU KNOW? The world's fourth largest center for human genome sequencing is located at the University of Oklahoma Advanced Center for Genome Technology.

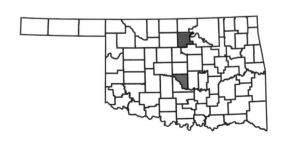

Pensacola Dam, LANGLEY ■

The Pensacola Dam is the first hydroelectric system in Oklahoma providing flood control for the counties along the Grand River. The Pensacola Dam is responsible for generating power for the Grand River Dam Authority, which provides electric service for 24 counties, plus many businesses both inside and outside Oklahoma.

> **I** am truly proud to be an Oklahoman. I was born in Gore, raised in Miami and have made my home in Norman for more than 30 years. I have raised my children here. The people of this great state are generous, supportive and have huge hearts. There isn't any other place I would rather live.
>
> **— STEVE OWENS**
> *University of Oklahoma Heisman Trophy winner, 1969*

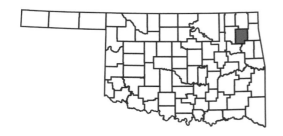

Oklahoma State Capitol Dome, OKLAHOMA CITY
True to the State's reputation for oil, Oklahoma is the
only state with a working oil rig on its capitol's property.

OG&E Windmill Farm, WOODWARD ■

The Oklahoma Wind Energy Center, located on 1,200 acres of ranchland 12 miles northeast of Woodward, became fully operational in 2003. The 68 huge GE wind turbines produce enough electricity for approximately 30,000 homes.

I have traveled all over the United States during my golf career, and Oklahoma is the place I call home. Oklahoma has the best, friendliest people with good values. It is a great place to raise your family.

— BOB TWAY
PGA Golfer

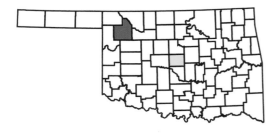

■ Weyerhaeuser Paper Mill, VALLIANT

This multibillion-dollar Fortune 200 company began producing forest products in Oklahoma in 1969. One year later, this containerboard mill opened and was the largest of its kind in the world.

DID YOU KNOW? Braum's Ice Cream and Dairy Stores owns its herds, seven farms and ranches, the processing plants, and 280 retail sites. It holds the title of "the world's only ice cream maker that milks its own cows."

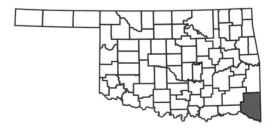

■ **City Meat Market, ERICK**

This is the oldest building in Erick—a western Oklahoma town founded in 1901. The Market once served Route 66 travelers, and local farm and ranch workers. Now, surrounded by many beautiful brick buildings on Erick's main street, it houses the Sand Hills Curiosity Shop.

DID YOU KNOW? Poultry, eggs and winter wheat make up Oklahoma's most valuable commodities.

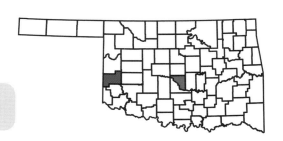

National Severe Storm Laboratory, NORMAN ■
Here, meteorologists, physicists, engineers and computer scientists research severe
weather and develop ground-breaking strategies for early storm detection and warning.

■ Wheat Harvest, KREMLIN

In approximately 9 seconds, this combine can harvest enough Oklahoma wheat to make 70 loaves of bread. The top cash crop in Oklahoma is hard red winter wheat. Oklahoma is typically the second-ranking state in winter wheat production, depending on the season.

Ditch Witch Factory, PERRY ■

The Ditch Witch Worldwide Headquarters is home to more than 1,300 employees of The Charles Machine Works, Inc. The company features a manufacturing plant nearly 30 acres in size. Additional on-site facilities house sales and marketing, training, testing, research, and product development.

■ **Bank of Oklahoma, TULSA**

The Bank of Oklahoma Tower, on the northern edge of downtown Tulsa, was completed in 1975. Designed by Minoru Yamasaki & Associates, the same architects who designed the World Trade Center (WTC) towers in New York City, the building is very similar, on a smaller scale, to a single tower from the WTC.

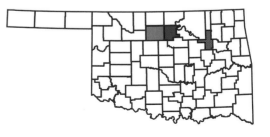

■ **Parker Drilling Company Rig 114, ELK CITY**
Standing at 181 feet, this is one of the tallest
and deepest-drilling rigs in the world.

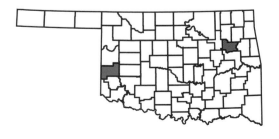

■ **Vance Air Force Base, ENID**

Vance Air Force Base is home to the 71st Flying Training Wing. Vance is the U.S. Air Force's only Joint Specialized Undergraduate Pilot Training base, training more than 400 Air Force, Navy, Marine Corps and allied student pilots for worldwide deployment and Aerospace Expeditionary Force Support in the T-1, T-6 and T-38 aircraft.

Federal Building, OKLAHOMA CITY ■

Just north of the former Alfred P. Murrah Federal Building is the new 180,000-square-foot Federal Building, housing various federal agencies. It sits on Federal Campus, which covers two city blocks.

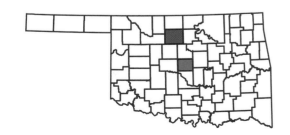

American Airlines Base, TULSA ■

The Tulsa Maintenance and Engineering Base employs more than 7,000 people. The Tulsa facility ranked as the world's largest aircraft maintenance base in 2005, largely due to American Airlines striving to keep most maintenance work in-house and to solicit work from other carriers.

■ Fire Fighting Training, Autry Technology Center, ENID

Autry Technology Center is part of a nationally acclaimed system of 29 technology centers with 54 campuses statewide. The centers develop a rich pool of skilled labor that helps businesses succeed in our state.

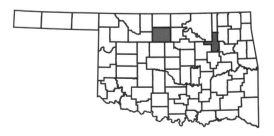

Oil Rig, CARNEGIE ■

This Oklahoma oil rig coexists easily with the surrounding agriculture. Oil has played a large role in Oklahoma's economy since the first commercial oil well was completed on April 15, 1897.

Sonic Headquarters, OKLAHOMA CITY ■

Headquartered in the state's capital, Sonic has seen tremendous growth since its inception in 1953 as a small drive-in restaurant in Shawnee. With more than 3,000 drive-ins across the United States and in Mexico, Sonic wins the title of "largest drive-in chain in the nation."

I have been fortunate enough to travel the country and see some amazing places, but there is always a reminder of what I miss back home. I have amazing memories of growing up in Oklahoma and am excited to see where my home state is headed. I'm proud to be an Oklahoman!

— **GRAHAM COLTON**
Singer

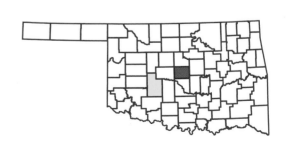

Train at Sunset, OKARCHE ■

DID YOU KNOW? Aerospace is the state's largest industry, employing more than 140,000 Oklahomans.

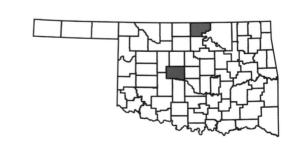

ConocoPhillips Refinery, PONCA CITY ■

ConocoPhillips is the second-largest refiner of petroleum products in the United States. The company's products are sold at 14,300 retail and wholesale outlets around the world, primarily under the Phillips 66, Conoco and 76 brands in the United States.

Covering Cotton Bales, ROOSEVELT ■
Before loading these cotton bales onto trucks en route to the gin, workers cover the bales to protect them from the elements.

I feel very lucky to have been born and raised in the state of Oklahoma. One of the greatest honors of my life was being inducted into the Oklahoma Sports Hall of Fame.

— DON HASKINS
Naismith Memorial Basketball Hall of Fame coach and subject of the movie "Glory Road"

Will Rogers World Airport, OKLAHOMA CITY ■

A recent $110 million expansion extends terminal space to nearly 600,000 square feet with a soaring 53-foot ceiling, and positions the airport within the top 10 in land area at 12 square miles.

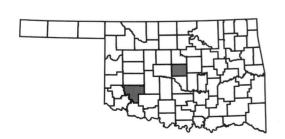

Oklahoma Department of Commerce, OKLAHOMA CITY
This Romanesque Revival style structure is home to the Oklahoma Department of Commerce. The 1907 building was expanded, keeping with the original architectural style, to provide nearly 40,000 square feet of space.

■ Administration Building, FORT SILL
Army buildings like this are a familiar sight in Fort Sill—a town and Army installation named for Brigadier General Joshua W. Sill, who served and died in the American Civil War.

Grain Elevator, RANCH DRIVE ■
High levels of wheat production give this area its reputation as the "Wheatheart of Oklahoma."

■ Bama Fried Pies, TULSA
Cinnamon dusts the signature fried pies at the Bama Companies, Inc. With production facilities in both Tulsa and Beijing, the company supplies customized bakery goods to casual dining markets throughout the world.

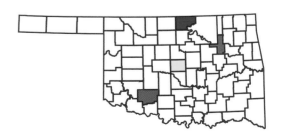

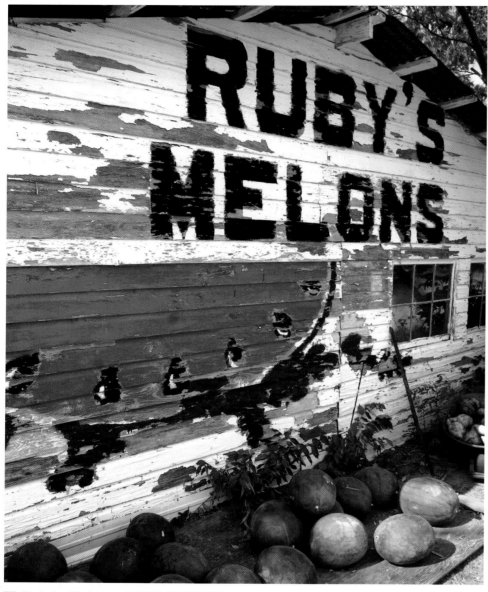

Farmers Market Pumpkins, OKLAHOMA CITY ■

Foal with Mother, Flyway Farm, ENID (right) ■
The Oklahoma horse industry is responsible for producing $762 million-worth of goods and services, and directly provides 14,500 full-time equivalent jobs.

■ **Ruby's Melons, RUSH SPRINGS**
Ruby's roadside fruit and vegetable stand provides juicy summer treats.

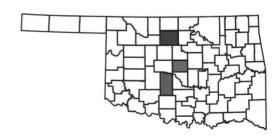

I have been fortunate to experience many places around the world, but my most celebrated journeys are those that bring me back to Oklahoma. There truly is no place like home.

— STACY PRAMMANASUDH
LPGA golfer

■ **Downtown, OKLAHOMA CITY**
Buildings of all shapes and sizes fill the city's estimated 115-block downtown.

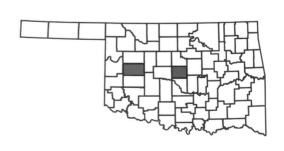

LEISURE

Living the Life

The hardscrabble pioneers who made our state a reality 100 years ago had lots of dreams.

Dreams of opportunity. Dreams of adventure. Dreams of somehow coaxing prosperity from a fertile but untamed land.

But one dream stood out from them all. The dream of experiencing life itself—in all its richness, all its fullness, all its energy and all its fun.

1

Oklahomans then—and Oklahomans now—know that life is for living. And our passion for living is nowhere more apparent than in the way we spend our leisure time. Soaking in the wondrous splendor of the creation. Experiencing adventure in the great outdoors. Testing physical talents through athletics—or cheering on those who do. And joining together with neighbors to celebrate a common heritage.

In Oklahoma, leisure isn't an escape; it's an affirmation of who we are and of what really matters.

To understand our people's thirst for living, you have to begin outdoors—on the land itself. A day hiking the scenic trails of the Wichita Mountains will be filled with gorgeous mountain scenery, diverse wildlife and lush green forests. The state's four major mountain ranges create exceptional camping, boating and fishing opportunities amid beautiful and diverse terrains. For example, nature-lovers often gravitate toward Turner Falls, located in the heart of the Arbuckle Mountains near Davis, where a 77-foot waterfall is surrounded by limestone caverns and natural caves in a 1,500-acre park.

If you want even more water, the crystal-clear lakes of eastern Oklahoma are a scuba-diver's delight.

1 Seventeenth Hole, Golf Club of Oklahoma, BROKEN ARROW

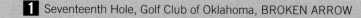

2 OSU Football, STILLWATER

And at Grand Lake O' the Cherokees in Grove, flocks of white pelicans sometimes make visitors feel as if they have been transported to an oceanside retreat. Those with a need for speed can thrill in motor-boating, sailing, waterskiing and personal watercraft rides on one of Oklahoma's 200 lakes. In fact, Oklahoma has more man-made lakes than any other state—as fishermen (and women) eager to cast a line can attest.

For many outdoor types, hunting is more than a cultural oddity that hearkens back to an earlier time; it is a present-day pursuit that offers year-round adventure and brings old and young together as one. Guided hunting tours throughout the state offer newcomers a chance to try their

hand. Oklahoma is also home to the nation's second-largest annual hunt, the Grand National Quail Hunt in Enid.

And yet, Oklahomans also know that the quiet of nature must sometimes be replaced with the roar of a crowd. And Oklahoma has plenty to offer on that front, as well. The University of Oklahoma and Oklahoma State University, the state's two Big 12 schools, have won multiple national championships in football, basketball, baseball and wrestling. In spring and summer, professional baseball beckons at the beautiful AT&T Bricktown Ballpark in Oklahoma City and Drillers Stadium in Tulsa, the largest Double A facility in the country. Oklahoma City's Blazers and

Tulsa's Oilers heat up the ice in fall and winter. Basketball fans can spend their winter and spring watching the NBA's "stars of tomorrow" play in its Development League team, the Tulsa 66ers. And summertime horse racing excites at tracks like Remington Park in Oklahoma City and Blue Ribbon Downs in Sallisaw.

1 Tulsa Raceway Park, TULSA

2 Grand Lake O' the Cherokees, GROVE

Dozens of private golf courses and more than 200 public courses tee up an entirely different kind of Oklahoma sporting life. Our claim to golfing fame starts with Tulsa's Southern Hills Country Club, which has hosted Professional Golf Association (PGA) Championships a record four times and the U.S. Open three times. Other first-class courses—including

Oak Tree, Karsten Creek and Gaillardia, among many others—have also welcomed PGA, LPGA and Senior tournaments.

Looking for wildlife? The family-friendly Oklahoma City Zoo's "Oklahoma Trails" exhibit is home to more than 800 native-Oklahoma animals in eight acres. The Tulsa Zoo and Living Museum was voted "America's Favorite Zoo" by Microsoft, and Norman's Little River Zoo promises a non-traditional zoo adventure for all visitors. Or get an up-close view of exotic rescued birds, reptiles and mammals (from cougars to the state's only known liger) at Safari's Sanctuary in Broken Arrow.

A "wild-at-heart" spirit also permeates our people. You can see it at Little Sahara State Park in northwestern Oklahoma, where buzzing ATVs and dune buggies race over sand dunes at breath-catching speeds. And Oklahoma's Wild West past lives on at more than one dozen Oklahoma guest ranches, as visitors from all over the world try activities ranging from cattle roping and butter churning to cowboy-song singing and chuck-wagon dining.

A party hat and dancing shoes also come in handy in the state. Gathering to commemorate, appreciate and celebrate is an Oklahoma forte, thanks to a host of festivals and historical events that recognize our diverse cultures and heritages.

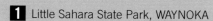
1 Little Sahara State Park, WAYNOKA

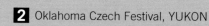
2 Oklahoma Czech Festival, YUKON

The Cherokee Strip Celebration in Enid honors the opening of the Cherokee Strip to settlers, and the Battlefire Civil War Re-enactment in Tribbey revisits the first Civil War battles in Indian Territory. With the sounds of pipes, drums and a Gaelic chorus drifting through the air, the Oklahoma Scottish Festival in Tulsa has brought a bit of Scotland to the Heartland since 1979. Oklahoma's largest multicultural event, the annual Global Oklahoma—A Festival of Cultures celebration in Midwest City is jam-packed with entertainment, art and ethnic foods. And each year, up to 250,000 people crowd the Arkansas River bank for "kartoffelpuffer" (potato pancakes) and other German foods at Tulsa's Oktoberfest—voted one of the

"top 10 places to harvest some fun" by *USA Today*. McAlester, the "Italian Capital of Oklahoma," hosts its annual Italian Festival, featuring authentic Italian food and activities, entertainment, and shopping.

And what's an authentic Italian meal without a glass of regional vino? Oklahoma boasts a surprising number of acclaimed wineries, many of which offer tours, tastings and harvesting opportunities.

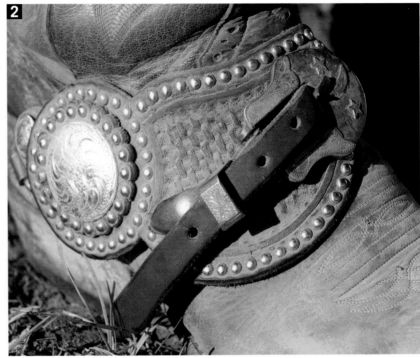

Do you want to live—to really live? Then come to Oklahoma. Our spectacular land invites exploration, adventure, excitement and relaxation. And our people have learned what really matters.

Just follow your heart … and name your pleasure. You're sure to find both here!

1 Buried Volkswagen, ARCADIA

2 Cowboy Boot, VICI

■ **Susan G. Komen Race for the Cure, OKLAHOMA CITY**
Thousands of Oklahomans have participated in the 5K and one-mile run annually for more than a decade. Proceeds benefit Oklahoma breast cancer patients, as well as the Komen Foundation Grant Program.

■ **Cherokee Queen II, Grand Lake O' the Cherokees, GROVE**

Sister ship to the Cherokee Queen, which launched in 1945, the Cherokee Queen II is equipped
with three decks and two dance floors. It can entertain 390 passengers during regular sight-seeing
tours, dinner and dance parties, holiday cruises, and private charter events.

DID YOU KNOW? Hunters, celebrities and top business leaders participate in Oklahoma's annual historic Grand National Quail Hunt—the leading celebrity hunting event in the nation.

■ **Native American Beads, Red Earth Festival, OKLAHOMA CITY**
The Red Earth Native American Cultural Festival is one of the largest celebrations of American Indian culture in the country. Members of more than 100 North American tribes gather to celebrate and share the richness and diversity of their proud heritage.

Garfield County Fair, ENID (right) ■

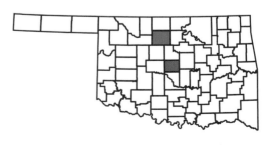

Quilting Hands, HENNESSEY ■
The art of quilting is a popular hobby—and livelihood—in many Oklahoma towns.

■ **Giraffe, Arbuckle Wilderness, DAVIS**
The Arbuckle Wilderness is a zoo-like park set on more than 400 acres of oak thickets and limestone outcroppings in the beautiful Arbuckle Mountains.

■ **Coleman Theatre Beautiful, MIAMI (left)**
Since its first show in 1929, this Louis XV venue has been entertaining audiences with events like ballets, pageants, organ concerts and operas.

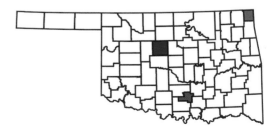

■ Cherokee Hotel and Casino, CATOOSA

The Cherokee Casino Resort Hotel opened in fall 2004. The hotel was designed with historical and cultural stylings taken from traditional Cherokee art, and its stunning art deco effects are reminiscent of historic downtown Tulsa.

> **O**klahoma is a land of music. I was immersed in it at church, school and with friends from my first memories of existence.
>
> **— JIMMY WEBB**
> *Grammy-winning composer, lyricist and performer*

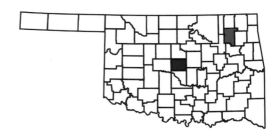

■ **Monkey, Little River Zoo, NORMAN**

This fascinated fellow was spotted at the Little River Zoo, which has educated and intrigued the public since 1996. The zoo offers personal tour guides for every guest and houses a wide variety of creatures—from exotic animals to abandoned pets.

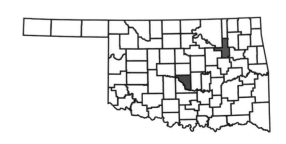

■ **Defense, University of Tulsa, TULSA (left)**

Mexican Rodeo, OKLAHOMA CITY

In traditional attire, this cowboy performs a rope trick at the city's Ford Center.
Other attractions include trick riding, Mariachi music and traditional dancing.

> **O**klahoma is the place I will always call home! Oklahoma is a state of great people perfectly embodying our American culture. I will always be grateful for the love, encouragement, prayers and support that I received from Oklahoma during my year of service as Miss America 1996. Happy Birthday, Oklahoma!
> — SHAWNTEL SMITH WUERCH
> *Miss America, 1996*

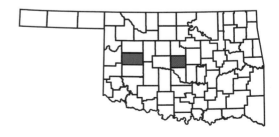

■ **Oklahoma Route 66 Museum, CLINTON**

This museum on historic Route 66 originally opened as the Museum of the Western Trails in 1968. An audio tour guides visitors through six decades of Route 66 history, focusing on transportation, culture and dining. Guests can purchase Route 66 mementos at the classic gift shop, which is stocked with videos, signs, toys and other collectibles.

DID YOU KNOW? Oklahoma offers two of the nation's select National Historic Trails.

■ Oklahoma Centennial Hot Air Balloon, TAHLEQUAH

■ 66 Bowl, OKLAHOMA CITY

Bowlers enjoy casual and competitive bowling on one of the 24 lanes at family-owned 66 Bowl on historic Route 66. Inside, guests can meet their bowling equipment needs at the 39th Street Emporium Pro Shop, or have some food and fun at the Silver Dollar Saloon.

Ford Center, OKLAHOMA CITY (right) ■

Home to the NBA Hornets during two seasons, this venue in downtown Oklahoma City is also home to the Oklahoma City Blazers hockey team and the Oklahoma City Yard Dawgz arena football team. In addition, the arena has hosted concerts by some top international acts, including The Who, the Rolling Stones and Billy Joel.

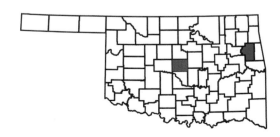

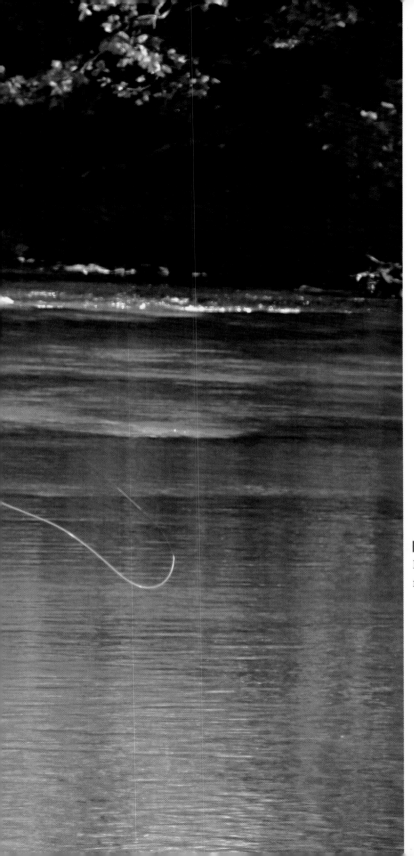

Oklahoma City Blazers Hockey Game, OKLAHOMA CITY ■

■ **Trout Fishing, BROKEN BOW LAKE (left)**
Beaver's Bend State Park on Broken Bow Lake is one of
many hot spots for trout fishing in southern Oklahoma.

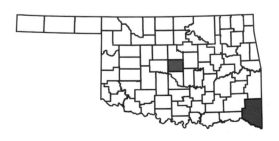

■ **Ice Skating, OKLAHOMA CITY**

Oklahoma families enjoy the ice—and the fun—at the
outdoor Braum's Skating Rink in downtown Oklahoma City.

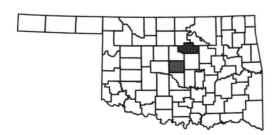

Bedlam Wrestling, STILLWATER (right) ■

Wrestlers from the University of Oklahoma and Oklahoma State
University do battle each year in the historic Bedlam series.

■ University of Oklahoma Football Game, NORMAN

The Gaylord Family-Oklahoma Memorial Stadium is packed on a fall Saturday. With a sold-out home crowd, more than 80,000 screaming Sooner fans make the stadium the sixth-largest "city" in Oklahoma for the afternoon.

OU Number 1!, NORMAN ■

Tradition holds that at each kickoff, University of Oklahoma fans symbolize number one with their index fingers and swiftly bring their arms down at the moment of the kick. Football is just one of OU's successful athletic teams. Altogether, Sooner athletic teams have earned more than 25 team national championships.

Oklahoma State University Flag, STILLWATER ■

This Cowboy waves the OSU flag from the end zone at Boone Pickens Stadium—renamed in 2003 for an OSU alumnus. The stadium's namesake recently donated $165 million to the school's athletic department, saying that athletics are a proven contributor to academic success.

■ **Oklahoma State University Football Crowd, STILLWATER**

Cowboy fans cheer in formation, proudly sporting their school colors as they spell "O-S-U."

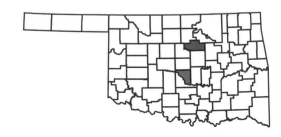

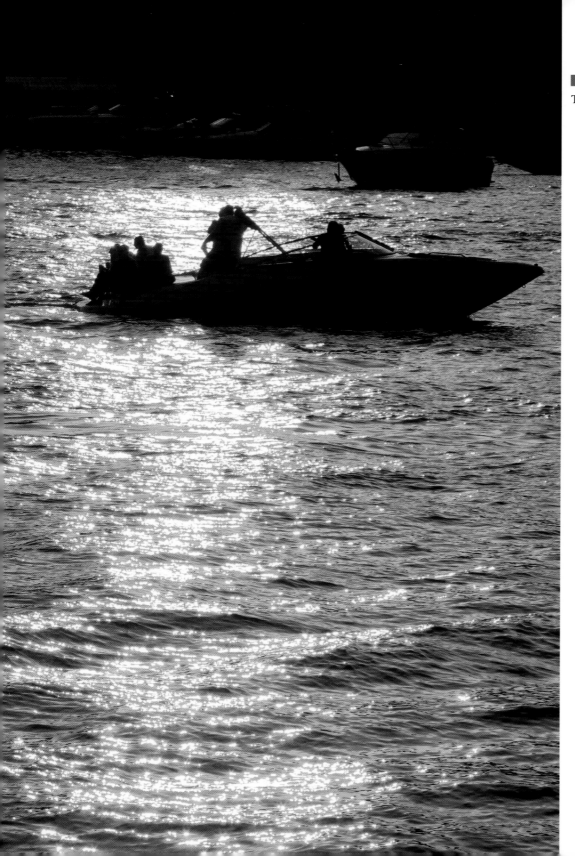

■ Evening, Grand Lake O' the Cherokees, GROVE
This lake's 46,500 surface acres of water are perfect for fishing, boating and water sports.

Oklahoma! Theme park of my youth ... ever up and running, carnival of wonderful and thunderful memories. I get to be a kid again when I think of or, even better yet, get back to Oklahoma.

— MASON WILLIAMS
Award-winning musician and writer

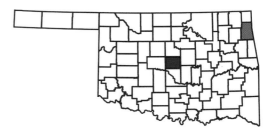

Fourth Hole, Oak Tree Golf Club, EDMOND
Host of the 70th PGA Championship in 1988, this private golf club draws enthusiasts to its Pete Dye-designed course.

NBA Hornets Basketball, OKLAHOMA CITY ■

For the Hornets, devastation from Hurricane Katrina meant a move from the New Orleans Arena to Oklahoma City's Ford Center for the majority of games during the 2005-06 and 2006-07 seasons. With a new set of "hometown" fans, the team's attendance grew substantially during its Oklahoma stay.

My Oklahoma roots grow deep. Both sets of grandparents came to Oklahoma to follow their dream of owning land and raising a family on their own farm. I, too, have seen dreams come true because of my rich Oklahoma heritage and abiding love of this land. We remain today a land of opportunity and blessings.

— JANE JAYROE
Miss America 1967

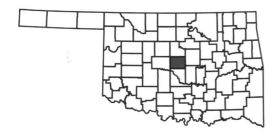

■ Oklahoma Aquarium, JENKS

The Oklahoma Aquarium, a public non-profit aquarium dedicated to conservation through education, is located on the banks of the Arkansas River in Jenks and brings an estimated half million visitors to the Tulsa area each year. The aquarium is home to more than 200 exhibits and the largest bull sharks in captivity in the world. Visitors of all ages can try their hand at feeding turtles, and get up close and personal with stingrays in the "touch tank."

■ Toy and Action Figure Museum, PAULS VALLEY

This unique museum pays tribute to the designers, sculptors and toy companies
that have turned action figures from children's playthings to works of art. Most
interesting are the behind-the-scenes looks at how these toys are made.

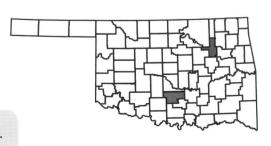

DID YOU KNOW? Guthrie's Scottish Rite Masonic Center is the world's largest Masonic building.

■ Junior Rodeo, BOISE CITY

Junior rodeo associations promote health, skill and good sportsmanship to young cowboys and cowgirls across Oklahoma.

Oklahoma is MORE than "OK"… it's a friend.

— **ROY CLARK**
Grammy-winning instrumentalist and entertainer

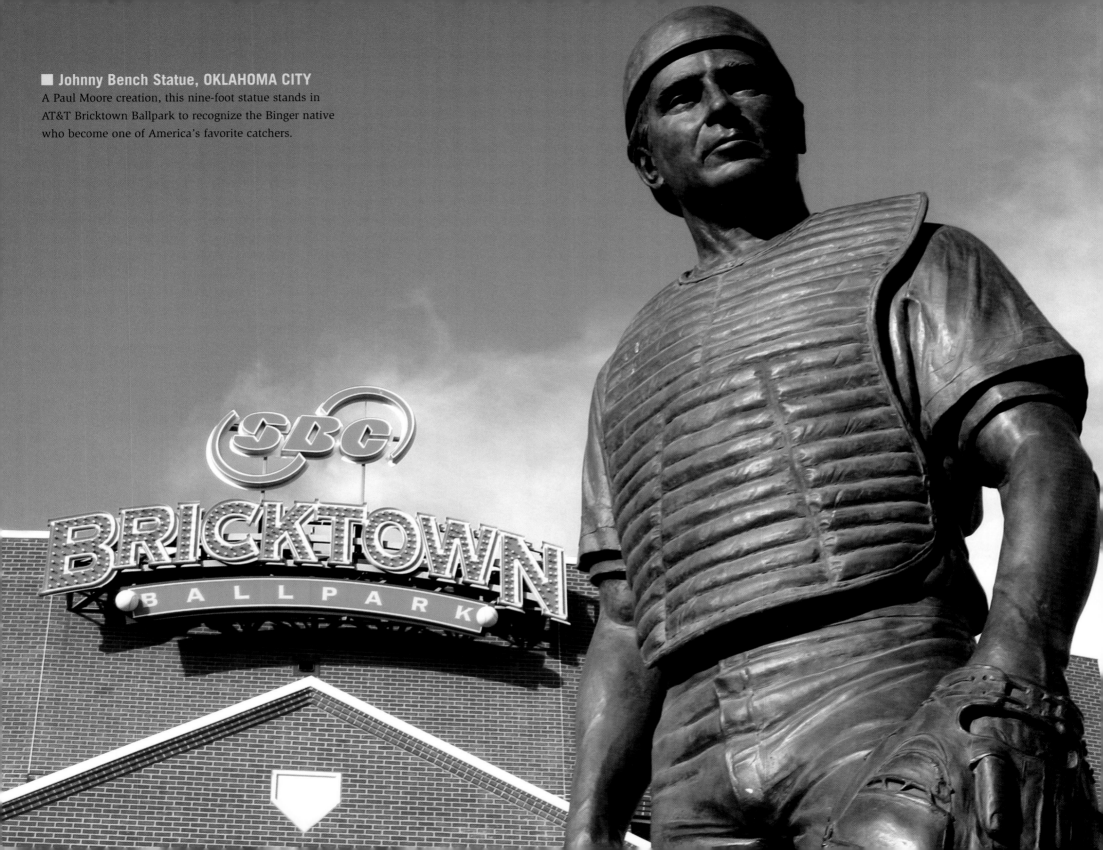

■ **Johnny Bench Statue, OKLAHOMA CITY**
A Paul Moore creation, this nine-foot statue stands in
AT&T Bricktown Ballpark to recognize the Binger native
who become one of America's favorite catchers.

Motocross Racer, ORLANDO ■

Motocross-lovers test their skill with "step-ups," "table tops" and "whoops" at more than one dozen extreme motocross parks throughout the state. And each year qualifiers from more than 100 motocross competitions in 33 states travel to Ponca City for the National Motosport Association Grand National Motocross Championship.

■ Bricktown, OKLAHOMA CITY (left)

A festive canal and river walk are two attractive elements in Oklahoma City's Bricktown. The area was revitalized in the 1980s and now includes countless attractions— from outdoor mosaics to sports arenas to art galleries. Bricktown is filled with places to dine, shop and socialize.

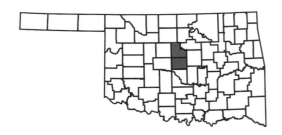

Banjo Player, Pawnee Bill Memorial Rodeo, PAWNEE ■

For three big nights every August, the Pawnee Bill Memorial Rodeo invites visitors to join a real cattle drive, ride in the wagon train, judge the chili and barbecue contests, buy some cowboy crafts, and enjoy rides and games—in addition to watching the rodeo.

DID YOU KNOW? The nation's largest collection of railroad artifacts is displayed at the Railroad Museum of Oklahoma in Enid.

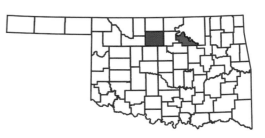

■ Canned Vegetables, ENID (left)

Food canning provides year-round nutrition in some Oklahoma households and is a popular competitive event at local and state fairs.

Three Riders, VICI ■

The Great Western Cattle Drive in Vici offers greenhorns and city slickers the chance to ride along with seasoned cowhands driving cattle as it was done in the 1800s. The South Canadian River Cattle Company was organized to provide an authentic cowboy adventure to tourists who have traveled from such faraway places as Canada, Germany and Japan.

■ **Horse and Rider, VICI**

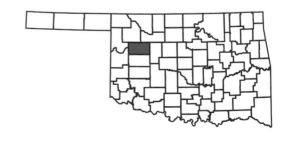

■ Cattle Drive, VICI

■ **Leonardo's Discovery Warehouse and Adventure Quest, ENID**

This hands-on museum in downtown Enid was conceived and designed by
a team of artists, scientists, children and educators. The community chipped
in with thousands of volunteer hours to help make this dream come true.

Tennis, TULSA ■

Tulsa is home to many outstanding tennis facilities but is best known for The University of Tulsa's Michael D. Case Tennis Center. Universally recognized as the finest collegiate tennis facility in the nation, it hosted the NCAA Division I Men's Tennis Championships in 2004 and is already booked for future NCAA tournaments.

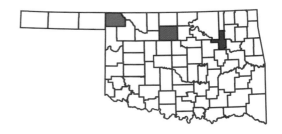

■ **Bats, SELMAN**

Summer nights bring forth a swarm of bats in Selman, the home of one of Oklahoma's largest bat "maternity colonies." Organized tours offer the chance to watch young bat pups stick close to their mothers as they hunt for dinner—a fine cuisine of mosquitoes, moths and beetles.

■ Solitary Rower, OKLAHOMA CITY

The newly revitalized Oklahoma River—including the
$3.5 million Chesapeake Boathouse—hosts nationally respected
rowing competitions, including dramatic night-racing events.

> **M**y home is Oklahoma. I have had the
> opportunity to travel the world with wrestling;
> I have been blessed with great success. I have been
> inspired and motivated by family, coaches, mentors,
> teachers, and many other Oklahomans throughout
> my journey. Through this I have come to understand
> that I live in the greatest place on Earth.
>
> **— JOHN SMITH**
> *Two-time Olympic Gold Medalist and
> Head Wrestling Coach, Oklahoma State University*

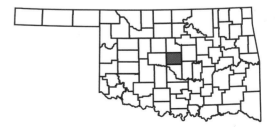

COMMUNITY

Caring, Giving and Persevering

Driving west from Stillwater on Highway 51, you'll soon leave rolling hills dotted with cedar trees and emerge onto Oklahoma's great high plains. It was here that millions of cattle marched across the state on the Great Western and Chisholm trails, moving up from Texas to railheads in Kansas, waiting to be shipped off to beef-hungry cities back east.

After a couple of hours, Highway 51 joins with Highway 60 and begins to curve north a bit, soon leveling out at the small town of Vici, Okla.

As you come in from the east, Vici (pronounced with a long "i" and the "s" sound) appears typical of many small Oklahoma

towns. Highway 60 becomes Broadway and is dotted with the obligatory few small buildings, the grain elevator, the bank and a couple of quick stops. The school sits off the main road in the southwest corner of town by the airport.

But just beneath its tranquil surface, Vici has a fascinating story to tell. It's a story about good citizens finding a way to keep their little town alive. It's also a story that illustrates what comes naturally in Oklahoma's communities. We're a generous, giving people who band together when times get tough.

On the north side of Broadway, about a block east of Main Street, sits Vici Grocery. The store has been

around for as long as anyone can remember, but with ownership changing every few years, it struggled to stay open. By 2004, Vici Grocery was up for sale again, but this time no potential buyers came calling.

And that was a problem. After all, this was the only grocery store in town. Sure, there were bigger stores in nearby Woodward, but driving 20 miles for groceries was not an option for many of Vici's older citizens. In addition, the town of Vici desperately needed the tax revenue a flourishing grocery store could provide. Something had to be done to keep this landmark from closing.

That's when a fierce community spirit began to rise up in the

1 Marland Estate, PONCA CITY

2 St. Paul's Catholic Church, MCALESTER

people of Vici. Rather than risk losing the store, a group of locals quickly organized as the VIP (Vici Investment People). These dedicated townspeople committed themselves to doing whatever it took to keep their grocery store from closing.

Eventually a buyer was found—but he didn't have enough money to make the purchase on his own. So, 20 VIPs put up $5,000 each to make the down payment on the store and allow the new buyer to take over. VIP saved the day ... and the store.

Unfortunately, their challenges were just beginning. When the new owner of the Vici Grocery told the investors he'd had enough—after only nine months—VIP faced yet

another crisis. Could they find a way to keep the store open or should they give up, walk away from their investment and perhaps lose the community they loved?

Like the early-day Sooners, they were brave enough to give it a try. The investors simply decided to run the store themselves—at least until a new buyer could be found.

Volunteers from all over town donated their time and hard work. They were at the store by dawn to sweep the aisles, wash the produce and receive the daily deliveries. They stayed at the store until late in the evening stocking the shelves, paying the bills and making the deposits. All were well aware what the store's closing could mean to the town—and they weren't going to let that happen.

After another backbreaking nine months, VIP found a new buyer to take over the store in July 2006. The investors were able to recoup close to 80 percent of their original investment. And today, the store is back on solid ground. With that

1 2 3

1 Tractor Crossing Sign, CARRIER

3 Pioneer Woman, PONCA CITY

2 Grocery Sign, PAULS VALLEY

accomplishment, you might think VIP members would kick back, fold their arms and call it a day. No way. The group is already looking for more investment opportunities in and around Vici to help keep the community strong.

That willingness to leap into the unknown and take on a big challenge is a familiar story to Oklahomans. In the early 1800s, only the bravest of souls would even attempt the journey to the

Indian Territories to put down roots and start a new life. Plenty of endurance and skill, mixed with a strong will to survive was required. Down through the years, those traits have intertwined to form a unique blend of perseverance, courage and loyalty known as the Oklahoma Spirit.

Oklahoma communities are populated with people who will not give in or give up. This Oklahoma Spirit can be found all across the state—in towns as varied as Ada and Avant, Guthrie and Gotebo, Slapout and Stigler, Lawton and Loco.

It is also found in our biggest city—Oklahoma City.

Like so many American cities, Oklahoma City's downtown was dying in the late 1970s. Dozens of buildings sat empty and decaying as an exodus to the suburbs left a shrinking downtown community. Dark warehouse windows stared blankly at the traffic on the interstates all going someplace else.

By the early 1980s, city leaders had seen enough. They weren't willing to sit back and watch this once vital area die. They aggressively pursued and encouraged businesses to come back to the area. They established tax credits for restoration projects.

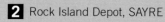

1 Wall Painting, ANADARKO

2 Rock Island Depot, SAYRE

They created a new identity—Bricktown—to attract potential investors and businesses. They imagined and soon built a canal that created a river walk to tie the entire area together.

Today, with a new downtown events arena and ballpark, dozens of restaurants, art galleries, shops, hotels, and other businesses, Bricktown is thriving. The area teems with tourists and visitors from all over the country, as well as with residents moving back to the area. From an empty warehouse district crisscrossed by railroad tracks, a new, vibrant community has come to life and made downtown Oklahoma City a desired destination.

The Spirit of Vici and Oklahoma City—and dozens of other Oklahoma communities—reflects the heart of yesterday's territorial settlers. Long before official statehood, adventurers, entrepreneurs and opportunists came to the Indian Territories to seek out a new life. Their covered wagons were packed with more than just their families and earthly belongings. These early Oklahomans knew they would need to forge strong ties with each other in order to survive life on the prairie. Although fiercely independent, they came together to establish robust communities—places where they could take advantage of their common strengths.

In the years since, Oklahomans have always been quick to answer the call for help in times of trouble—rushing in with

food and clothing, medical supplies, or much-needed financial assistance. That's what neighbors do.

That's the Spirit of our state's towns and cities. Caring. Giving. Persevering. Growing. In Oklahoma, we know that "community" isn't just a word. It's a value that defines who we are.

1 The Indian Lodge, WAGONER

2 Giant Chickens, DRUMMOND

■ **Cherokee National Capital, TAHLEQUAH**

The Cherokee Council first met in this location in 1839 under a large open shed. The Council later assembled in log buildings, which were burned to the ground during the Civil War. After the war, the Council made provisions for a new building. It was built on this site and occupied in 1870.

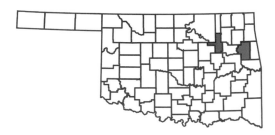

Centennial Kickoff Celebration, TULSA (right) ■

Tulsa opened Oklahoma's year-long Centennial celebration with a bang as its downtown skyline played stage to a colorful bazaar of sights and sounds. Musically choreographed fireworks and lasers accompanied inspirational Oklahoma images, which were projected onto several 200-foot building-mounted screens.

■ Eskimo Joe's, STILLWATER

Stillwater's Jumpin' Little Juke Joint was opened in 1975 by Steve File and Stan Clark. They launched the original location as a bar but converted it to a full-service restaurant in 1984. What really put Eskimo Joe's on the map were their t-shirts emblazoned with Bill Thompson's original logo design featuring Eskimo Joe and his faithful dog, Buffy. Next to Oklahoma State University football, nothing draws a bigger crowd in Stillwater than the restaurant's annual anniversary bash, held every July on Elm Street in front of the restaurant.

DID YOU KNOW? Oklahoma ranks 37th in the nation in per capita income, but is sixth in giving.

Poncan Theatre, PONCA CITY ■

Since 1927, this venue has offered everything from live performances to silent features with organ accompaniment. After the Spanish Colonial Revival theatre closed in 1985, the community rallied around it, planning its restoration and reopening the building in 1994.

I t was a great privilege for me to look down at Oklahoma from about 435 km above the earth. What took my grandfather a full day to traverse with his horse and wagon with supplies, we took less than five seconds to cover in an orbiting spacecraft! And all this was accomplished in less than the first 70 years of the Age of Aviation and Space. It is still mind-boggling to me!

— **OWEN K. GARRIOTT**
Former NASA astronaut

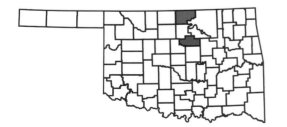

■ Dewey Hotel Museum, DEWEY

This 1899 Victorian hotel has undergone renovations and is now open for tours, during which visitors can view the antique interiors and beautiful period pieces.

4-H Goat Show, ENID ■

4-H is a national leadership-building organization with chapters throughout Oklahoma.

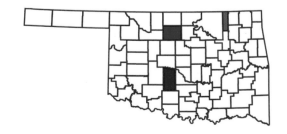

■ Train Depot, CHICKASHA

My basic feeling about our state is one of pride. Pride in the way three generations converted what was largely wilderness into a space-age society. Proud of the way our citizens survived The Great Depression. Proud of the way a generation served in the military during WWII and distinguished themselves in battle. Proud of a new generation that has adapted to the high-tech world and proud of the way our state is preparing for a new century.

— HENRY BELLMON
Former State Representative and Senator, two-time Governor and two-term U.S. Senator

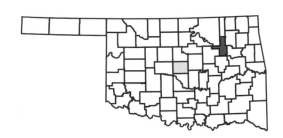

Golden Driller, TULSA ■

The largest freestanding statue in the world, this 76-foot giant has proudly guarded Tulsa's Expo Center since 1966. Its inscription reads: "The Golden Driller, a symbol of the International Petroleum Exposition. Dedicated to the men of the petroleum industry who by their vision and daring have created from God's abundance a better life for mankind."

■ Downtown Skyline, **OKLAHOMA CITY**

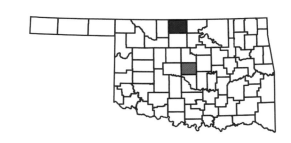

DID YOU KNOW? | The University of Oklahoma has the nation's highest per capita enrollment of National Merit Scholars.

■ Red Round Barn, POND CREEK

This round barn sits on a farm along the Salt Fork of the Arkansas River in Grant County.

■ Sante Fe Train Depot, SHAWNEE

■ Chamber of Commerce, PERRY

This distinctive building, now home of the Perry Chamber of Commerce, is the century-old product of French designer Joseph Foucart, who immigrated to America in 1888 following his service in the Franco-Prussian War. With its artistic brick and stonework, embossed interior ceilings, and trademark horseshoe window, this building is estimated to have cost $7,500 to complete—a small fortune in 1902.

Neighborhood Sign, KETCHUM ■

Lake neighborhoods take on their own unique personalities.
This sign near Ketchum points the way home for several families.

I'm so proud to be from Oklahoma, and to be the goodwill ambassador and official comedian of the Oklahoma Centennial. The people of my hometown, Ponca City, recently honored me with a marker in front of the house where I was raised on Parkview Drive. The sign reads "Stillwater—38 miles."

— ARGUS HAMILTON
Comedian and columnist

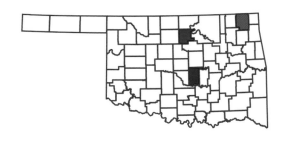

■ **Mickey Mantle Field, COMMERCE**

Although Mickey Mantle was born in nearby Spavinaw, he called Commerce home. Mantle was a three-sport star for Commerce High and was even offered a football scholarship to the University of Oklahoma. But Mantle's true love was baseball, and he signed his first pro contract with the New York Yankees' Class D team in Independence, Kansas, on the day he graduated from high school in 1949. This ball field in Commerce bears his name.

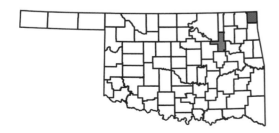

CityPlex Towers, TULSA (right) ■
This beautiful three-tower office complex boasts
more than 2 million square feet of space.

■ Lew Wentz Swimming Pool, PONCA CITY
This public pool is part of the Lew Wentz Camp and Pool built by Oklahoma oilman and philanthropist Lew Wentz.

I wasn't born in Oklahoma. I arrived when I was 12 and only lived in the Sooner state until I was 19. But those seven years spent in a small rural town in the eastern part of the state formed the strong foundation of my life—not only in education and sports, but in lifelong friendships. I'm as proud to say today as I did when I graduated from high school: I'm from Henryetta, Oklahoma!

— TROY AIKMAN
Former University of Oklahoma and Dallas Cowboys quarterback

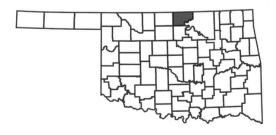

Woody Guthrie Mural, OKEMAH ■

A legend recognized for his great impact on the development of folk music, Woody Guthrie hailed from the heartland town of Okemah. His survival of The Great Depression, the Great Dust Storm, World War II and personal tragedies sowed a rich field from which he produced poetry and prose, a novel, and more than 1,000 songs. Over his 55-year life, Guthrie inspired countless songwriters, received the U.S. Department of the Interior's Conservation Service Award and was inducted into the Songwriters Hall of Fame.

■ **Slide, State Fair Park, OKLAHOMA CITY (left)**

Rides like this giant slide are only part of what families enjoy at the Oklahoma State Fair. Plenty of food, livestock shows, creative arts contests, shopping opportunities and musical entertainment means fun for everyone.

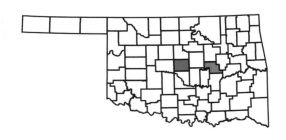

■ **Dairy Sweet Drive-In, COVINGTON**

Drive-ins are a common sight in small towns all across Oklahoma
and often serve as the hub of the community. This one has become
a favorite hangout over the years for old and young alike.

DID YOU KNOW? More than 80,000 plots of Oklahoma acreage—over 70 percent of the state—are occupied by farms and ranches.

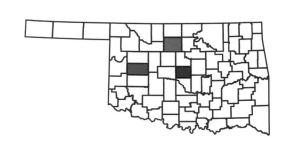

Skirvin Hotel, OKLAHOMA CITY ■

After sitting vacant for nearly two decades, a $55 million renovation restored splendor to the Skirvin—the namesake hotel of Oklahoma oilman William "Bill" Skirvin. This 14-story attraction has long been popular with celebrities from around the world.

■ **McPhetridge Centennial Park, WEATHERFORD**

The park, built on the historic site of Weatherford's first bank, was completed in 1997 to commemorate the town's 100th birthday. Walkways are paved with centennial bricks donated by city residents, businesses and organizations. The gazebo, fountain, landscaping and time capsule welcome visitors to this historic location at the corner of Main Street and Broadway.

Yukon Mill and Grain Company, YUKON ■

Housing grain since the late 1800s and shipping overseas by 1915, the historic Yukon Mill plays an important role in the production and shipment of feeds and flour.

Familiar Icon, OKLAHOMA CITY ■

This Braum's bottle tops a French-Vietnamese bakery called Saigon Baguette, which is tucked into an interesting triangular brick building.

It is a privilege to coach at the University of Oklahoma because of the sense of pride Oklahomans feel for the traditional success of this program. We are grateful for that outpouring and very much aware that this program represents a lot more to our state than just the sport alone.

— BOB STOOPS
Head Football Coach, University of Oklahoma

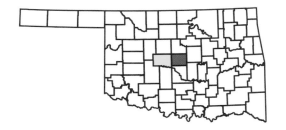

■ Kiowa County Courthouse, HOBART

This building, designed by J. Riley Gordon, was constructed in 1902 in the Neoclassical and Second Renaissance Revival architectural style popular during that time. In the foreground, one can see a ceramic tile map of southwestern Oklahoma that enables visitors to actually walk "across" the state.

Beckham County Courthouse, SAYRE ■

One may recognize this building from the film, "The Grapes of Wrath," but locals know it as the Beckham County Courthouse. The 1911 building was added to the National Register of Historic Places in 1984.

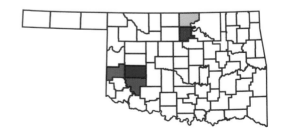

Kay County Courthouse, NEWKIRK ■

Kay County borders Kansas and is located in the north central part of the state. The original courthouse, which was built in 1894, was replaced in 1926 with this stone building. Kay County is the only county in the state to keep its name ("K" County) through the transition from Indian Territory to statehood.

■ **Washita County Courthouse, CORDELL**

This stately building is recognized on the National Register of Historic Places for its Classical Revival architecture. The surrounding area, New Cordell Courthouse Square Historic District, dates back to 1875 and was added to the Registry in 1999.

Noble County Courthouse, PERRY ■

Courthouse Square is the center of downtown Perry. Built in 1916, the three-story courthouse provides office space for county officials and houses the Noble County jail in a rooftop super-structure. This bronze statue, "Hopes and Dreams," was installed on the east lawn of the courthouse park in 1993, during the Cherokee Strip Centennial.

■ **Overstreet-Kerr Historical Farm, SALLISAW**
This estate dates back to 1895 and is listed on the National Register of Historic Places. Sitting on 3,000 acres of farmland, the 15-room home was restored to its original beauty in 1991 and is now open for tours.

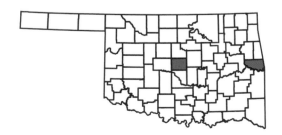

Hillbillee's Café and Bed & Breakfast, ARCADIA (right) ■
From an old Phillips 66 filling station and motor lodge to a self-proclaimed "Hillbillee Heaven," this inviting bed-and-breakfast draws hungry travelers with its delicious home cooking, live music and Oklahoma fun. Hillbillee's Café has been serving up its famous fried chicken and cobbler on historic Route 66 since 1993.

Rattlesnake Roundup, OKEENE ▪

The annual summertime three-day Rattlesnake Roundup provides fun for licensed hunters as they search out serpents for cash prizes. Those preferring less dangerous adventure enjoy the festival's train rides, community dances and finger-licking food, including rattlesnake.

■ Uniform, First American Boy Scout Troop, PAWHUSKA

The very first Boy Scout troop in America was organized in Pawhuska in 1909 by Rev. John F. Mitchell, a missionary priest from England. Rev. Mitchell organized Troop 1 under English charter and equipped the 19 charter members with manuals and uniforms like this one, from England.

> **I**f I had all the money in the world, I'd live in Oklahoma ... I love Oklahoma! I love the people! I love you ... pass it on!
>
> **— DANNY WILLIAMS**
> *Radio/television personality*

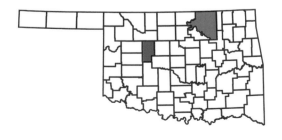

■ Bell Tower, BEAVER

The town of Beaver is the county seat of Beaver County and host to the annual World Champion Cow Chip Throw each April. The world record was set in 1979 by Leland Searcy. He heaved the chip just over 182 feet.

DID YOU KNOW? In the Arbuckle Mountains, Falls Creek Baptist Encampment is the largest religious encampment in the world, with more than 45,000 guests each summer.

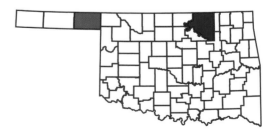

■ Triangle Building, PAWHUSKA

This rare, freestanding triangle building was built in 1915 to fill a triangular piece of land left in the middle of town after early buildings had been constructed. In the Oil Boom days, the building housed more than 100 lawyers.

■ **Elephants, HUGO**
The Endangered Ark Foundation houses the second-
largest population of elephants in the nation.

Mural, HUGO ■
This happy clown jazzes up a local circus truck.

Elephant Band Drum, HUGO ■

Props like this decorated drum have helped Carson and Barnes Circus captivate crowds since the late 1930s. Carson and Barnes is one of several circuses that winter in Hugo.

■ Showmen's Rest, HUGO

This tombstone marks one of many circus people and bull riders peacefully laid to rest in the section of Mt. Olivet Cemetery known as "Showmen's Rest." Other markers reflect the extravagance of the lives they honor with elephant-shaped monuments and circus etchings.

■ **Chamber of Commerce, WAGONER**

Purchased in 1995, the home of Wagoner's Chamber of Commerce was originally a movie theater. The building, complete with a gymnasium and kitchen, still houses musical shows and movies in the original theater.

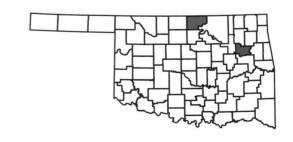

Marland Estate, PONCA CITY ■

Former home of Oklahoma governor and oil baron E.W. Marland, this four-level, 43,561-square-foot mansion has 55 rooms, a working Otis elevator from 1926 and one of the first saunas in the nation. Rising from dire financial losses, E.W. Marland made several oil discoveries, through which he gained control of one-tenth of the world's oil by 1922. Ponca City purchased the mansion in 1975, and daily tours captivate visitors with the exceptional sculpture, artwork, architecture and history of the 1925 structure.

In 1981, when I was 5 years old in Elk City, Oklahoma, Susan Powell (native Elk Citian) became Miss America. She was studying with Florence Birdwell at OCU at the time. So, right then and there, I vowed to go to OCU one day and study with the "bird-lady," too. The rest is history ... my history, at least.

— KELLI O'HARA
Tony-nominated actress

WARES RANCH
BROWN RANCH
COWBOY CEMETERY

Road Signs, WOODS COUNTY ■

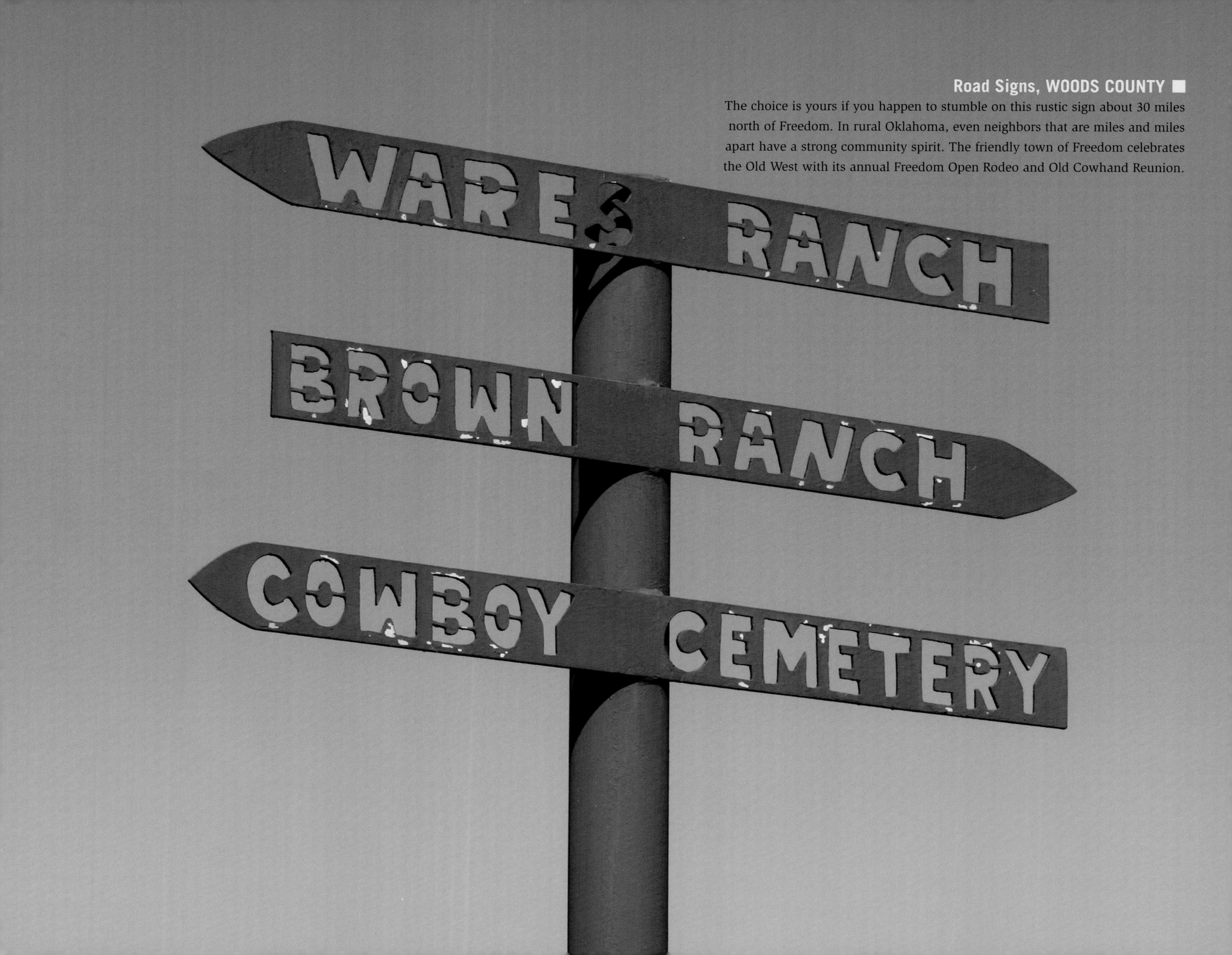

The choice is yours if you happen to stumble on this rustic sign about 30 miles north of Freedom. In rural Oklahoma, even neighbors that are miles and miles apart have a strong community spirit. The friendly town of Freedom celebrates the Old West with its annual Freedom Open Rodeo and Old Cowhand Reunion.

Frank Phillips Historic Home, BARTLESVILLE ■
Oilman Frank Phillips moved to Bartlesville eight years after the establishment of the state's first commercial oil well. A rocky business beginning quickly transformed into more than 80 successful oil wells, which provided the funds for this magnificent 1909 Neoclassical structure where Phillips carried out his business and philanthropic endeavors until his death in 1950.

■ **Hometown Star, CHECOTAH**
The community rallied behind their hometown heroine with billboards like this. From her eastern-Oklahoma hometown, Carrie Underwood sang her way to the top, winning the title of "American Idol" in 2005 and more recently the Country Music Awards' "Female Vocalist of the Year."

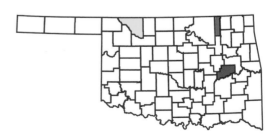

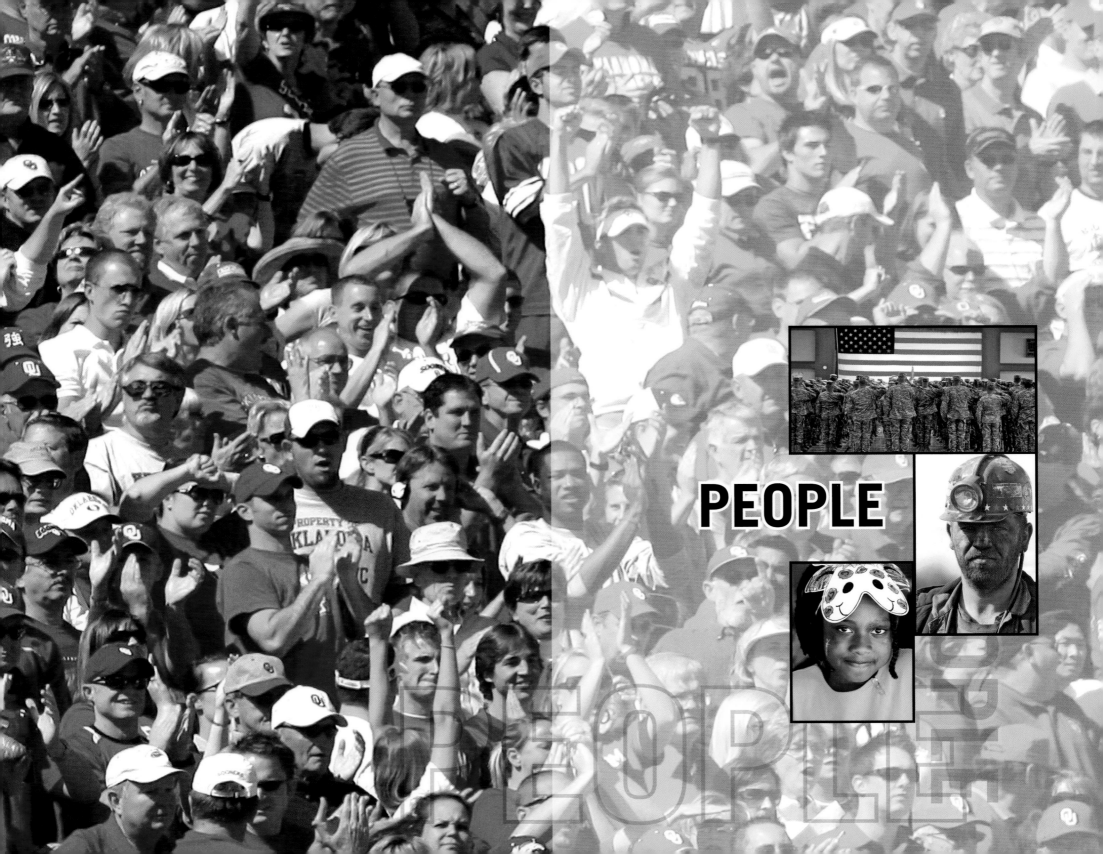

PEOPLE

"Hey! Where you from?"

This phrase—or something like it—has been a common greeting since man first started traveling from the place of his birth to parts unknown. We ask the question because we want context. We want to better understand, grasp or categorize the essence of another person. Knowing where the person is from helps us do just that.

But being from a place is more than a matter of mere geography. It reflects a connection to the land that made you ... the values that helped form you. It's your place of beginning, your point of origin, your genesis. The soil that brought you forth can't help but flavor the life you're destined to live.

Being from Oklahoma gives you a special distinction. It means you're an Okie, tied forever to past Oklahomans. It means you're a Sooner, linked with the "enterprising" souls who jumped the gun during the Land Run to claim the best plots of land "sooner" than anyone else. Though these terms were originally meant derisively, today Oklahomans wear these labels with pride: *"I'm proud to be an Okie from Muskogee!"* and *"I'm Sooner born and Sooner bred, and when I die, I'll be Sooner dead!"*

There's a greatness in this state of ours. It's evident in our art and athletics, in our communities and commerce, in our landscapes and history. But nowhere does this greatness shine like it does in our people.

Some famous Oklahomans stand out as obviously great men and women who have changed our world for the better. One might start with the wit and wisdom of our native son Will Rogers, born in the Cherokee Nation (near present day Oologah). But there's also the athletic prowess of Jim Thorpe, born in a one-room cabin near Prague ... the political genius of Carl Albert, the "Little Giant from Little Dixie" ... the majestic music of Woody Guthrie from Okemah ... and the leadership of Wilma Mankiller (the first female principal chief of the great Cherokee Nation), born in Tahlequah.

Many more lesser-known Oklahomans have also changed their world. Far too many to count. There's simply no way to chronicle all the human achievement this grand state has produced. Oklahomans, with their natural sense

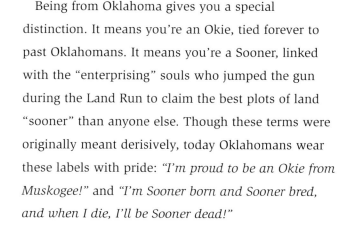

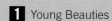
1 Young Beauties

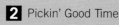
2 Pickin' Good Time

of curiosity, their creative genius and their gift for ingenuity, have forever impacted our world for the better.

Since a complete list isn't feasible, a few stories will have to suffice.

Take the story of Sylvan Goldman. Goldman was a man with a problem. Shoppers in his Oklahoma City grocery store weren't buying enough groceries. It wasn't that they bought all they needed. It was that they could buy only what they could carry. He needed a way to help those shoppers carry more and, therefore, buy more.

Working late one night in 1936, Goldman noticed two ordinary wooden folding chairs sitting in the

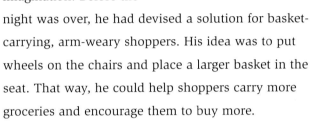

corner of his office. As he stared at those chairs, an idea began to take shape in his imagination. Before the night was over, he had devised a solution for basket-carrying, arm-weary shoppers. His idea was to put wheels on the chairs and place a larger basket in the seat. That way, he could help shoppers carry more groceries and encourage them to buy more.

Using the basic design of the folding chairs, Goldman—with help from Fred Young, one of the grocery store's maintenance men—invented the modern shopping cart. Inspired by two simple folding chairs, they built a cart with a metal frame and added wheels and wire baskets.

Goldman's natural Sooner curiosity led to an idea that revolutionized retail shopping. From small beginnings in one little grocery chain in

Oklahoma City, more than 30 million carts are used today in stores all over the United States, with more than one million new carts manufactured every year.

1 A Clever Disguise

2 Brave Warrior

Some of the most creative of Oklahoma ideas have come from the most unlikely places—even the funny pages.

In 1907, Oklahoma became the 46th state of the Union. That same year, a seven-year-old boy in Pawnee discovered the newspaper comics. Before long, he was trying to copy the simple strips, tracing the drawings he saw in the newspaper. Soon he was making up and drawing his own strips.

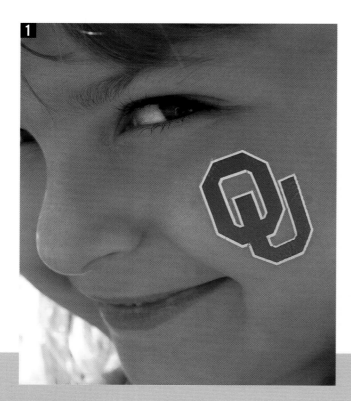

The boy grew up and attended Oklahoma A&M (now Oklahoma State University) in Stillwater, where he was hired by the *Daily Oklahoman* to draw a cartoon about athletes in the news. The cartoon was a local hit. Full of his newfound success, the young man left Stillwater and headed north to fulfill his dream of becoming a cartoonist for the *Chicago Tribune*.

That dream wasn't realized quickly. For 10 long years, the young man submitted one comic strip idea after another and received one rejection after another. Finally, the *Trib*'s editor found an idea he liked—a concept about a plainclothes crime fighter named Dick Tracy.

The illustrator's name was Chester Gould.

Gould's Oklahoma-bred creativity produced one of the most famous comic strips in history. Perhaps even more importantly, his foresight has led to many crime-fighting tools now routinely used by modern law enforcement. Today's wireless communications, portable surveillance cameras and caller ID technologies were all first seen in the Dick Tracy comic strip, dreamed up in the fertile imagination of Chester Gould.

Today, Pawnee honors the creativity of its native son with a huge mural on the side of a building at the corner of 6th and Harrison

1 Sooner Spirit

2 Go Pokes!

streets. The mural features Dick Tracy reminding us all that "Crime Does Not Pay."

For another example of true Sooner ingenuity, you need look no further than Ed Malzahn of Perry. Ed grew up in Perry as the grandson of the founder of a blacksmith shop. By the time Ed was a young man, his father, Charlie, was running the business, then known as Charlie's Machine Shop.

A smart businessman in his own right, Charlie asked Ed to think of something for the employees to do when they were not engaged in their normal work of making repairs to equipment in the nearby oil fields. Ed's thoughts quickly turned to a scene he had recently witnessed—

two men grunting, groaning and working up a heavy sweat as they struggled to break through rock in an attempt to dig a short utility ditch. Using his natural ingenuity, Ed came up with the idea for a small trencher. With his dad's assistance, he soon made the very first Ditch Witch.

Today, Ed is the CEO of The Charles Machine Works. He's still in Perry. But his innovative Ditch Witch machines are found all over the world and have been recognized as one of the 100 best American-made products in the world by *Fortune* magazine. All this from a resourceful guy in Perry with an idea of how to dig ditches easier and faster.

Sylvan Goldman, Chester Gould, Ed Malzahn … all Oklahomans whose curiosity, creativity, ingenuity and undeniable

commitment to hard work have helped change the world. These are the characteristics found in the heart and the soul of the people of our state.

As an Oklahoman, you carry the red earth of this state in your blood. When you hear the state song, you know it's YOUR sky the hawk is making lazy circles in. No matter where you may go, no matter how far you may travel—and just like countless others before you—you can be proud to say, "I'm from Oklahoma!"

1 Riding Home After the Game   **3** Joy

2 Handlebar

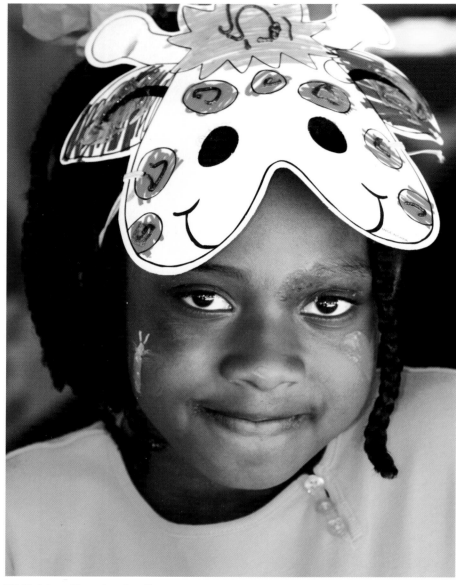

■ Taking Part in the Fun

Native American Veteran ■

An Oklahoma Smile (right) ■

Cowboy Fans ■

■ Young Amigo

Nice Hairdo ■

The "Salt of the Earth" people are what make Oklahoma great. A wonderful place to raise a family and feel very comfortable.

— MIKE GUNDY
Head Football Coach, Oklahoma State University

Summer Fun ■

■ Leather Tooling—Both Art and Industry

■ Solitude (left)

■ On the Range

Going to School ■

There is something special about a place where doctors, lawyers and entrepreneurs share a table at a local restaurant with cowboys, farmers and ranchers. That place is Oklahoma ... and the common bond is shared respect of family, faith and flag. Okie through and through ... and proud of it.

— TOMMY R. FRANKS
U.S. Army General (ret.)

■ Tradition Begins at a Young Age

Working the Land ■

■ Embracing Heritage

Is It Nap Time Yet? ■

DID YOU KNOW? Oklahoma has produced six Miss Americas.

Coal Miner: A Hard Day's Work ■

■ Party Time

Red, White and Blue ■

> **W**e have always been proud of Oklahoma and Tulsa's rich and rugged history, its great musical heritage, and the attributes of raw courage, leadership and philanthropy that characterize its history. We hope to be part of a generation that draws strength from those achievements, but also hungers to raise the bar and make the next 100 years better than the last.
>
> **— ISAAC, TAYLOR AND ZAC HANSON**
> *Musicians*

■ "Pawnee Bill"—High Style in the Midwest

A Grandmother's Love ■

■ Celebrating Czech Culture

■ The Joys of Summer

Prison Rodeo—Waiting to Ride ■

They came, they struggled and they prevailed. That could be any person's story who settled early day Oklahoma. Conditions were often harsh and unforgiving. But those wonderful people instilled in those of us who came later a love of land, brother and sister, and a solid belief that all things are possible as long as we do what must be done.

— GARY ENGLAND
Doppler Radar developer and Chief Meteorologist, KWTV

■ Together Again

Every unit returning to Lawton's Fort Sill from overseas duty receives a hometown greeting—with flags, tears and a community's heartfelt thanks.

| DID YOU KNOW? | With 39 tribes represented, Oklahoma has the most diverse Native American population in the country. |

Welcome Home ■

■ **A Wild Ride**

■ **Nervous but Happy**

Practicing for the Parade ■

■ **Native American Traditional Dance**

DID YOU KNOW? Oklahoma State University's familiar mascot, "Pistol Pete," with his handlebar mustache and leather chaps, is fashioned after author and U.S. Deputy Marshall Frank Eaton (b.1860).

Spanish Honor (right) ■

■ **Blow That Horn**

Weatherford was a wonderful place to grow up. The town was very nurturing. One of the real advantages I've had in my life was growing up in a small town in western Oklahoma.

— **THOMAS P. STAFFORD**
Former NASA Astronaut and U.S. Air Force Lieutenant General (ret.)

■ Technology Goes West

The Captain ■

When I made the decision to attend Oklahoma A&M and play basketball for Mr. Iba, I became an Oklahoman. In spirit, I never left. As we moved from state to state, the one constant was an Oklahoma newspaper in the mailbox every day. I love this state, so the opportunity to move back was a dream come true.

— EDDIE SUTTON
Former Head Basketball Coach, Oklahoma State University

■ Work Starts Early on a Cotton Farm

A Swinging Good Time ■

When I am asked to describe myself, I always begin by saying with deep pride that I am an Oklahoman. Oklahoma has kept alive the spirit of America. Oklahoma is a place where people truly care about each other and take care of each other. Oklahomans share a belief that the future will be better than the present, because they have an unmatched tenacity to make it happen.

— DAVID BOREN
University of Oklahoma President, former Governor and U.S. Senator

■ Kids Will Be Kids

■ Spanish Immersion Class (left)

■ **Working Hard**

| DID YOU KNOW? | Oklahomans' per capita personal income growth rate is the third highest in the nation. |

■ "O ... S ... U!"

When I left California, I could have moved to any place I wanted, but I came back to Oklahoma because I was always happier here—more than anyplace I have ever been.
— DALE ROBERTSON
Actor

■ **Hog Heaven (left)**

SUSTAINING SPONSORS

In an Oklahoma oil field in 1958, Claire Simmons and Carl White introduced the first Auto Crane from the trunk of a car. Nearly a half-century later, Auto Crane Company remains a global market leader, serving oil and natural gas, heavy construction, mining, and utility markets worldwide.

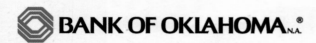

Bank of Oklahoma is a subsidiary of BOK Financial Corp., a leading $18.1 billion regional financial services company that has enjoyed 16 consecutive years of record earnings. Headquartered in Tulsa, BOKF has seven bank subsidiaries and 160 locations in eight states. It provides consumer banking, commercial banking and also offers a range of wealth management services nationwide.

Chickasaws have played a vital role in Oklahoma's dynamic history. Today, we celebrate the blending of cultures, innovative attitude and indomitable spirit that make Oklahoma great. Explore Native American history at our beautifully restored Chickasaw Capitol Building in Tishomingo. Nearby, enjoy exciting gaming facilities and the Bedré gourmet chocolate factory.

Cobb Engineering has served the engineering needs of Oklahoma citizens and communities since 1921. It's been a privilege to share both our professional services and valuable people with the state—an investment in Oklahoma's future that's marked by excellence, and measured through employees who embody Oklahoma's heritage, culture and ingenuity.

In 1893, after making the Cherokee Strip Land Run, W.B. Johnston established Johnston Enterprises, the state's oldest grain and seed company. More than a century later, the family-owned business continues a proud tradition, expanding operations to include two ports on the McClellan-Kerr Navigation System in Oklahoma and two in Louisiana.

Founded in 1901, Lawton is the state's third largest metropolitan area—a regional center for agricultural retail and distribution, manufacturing, processing, education, and recreation. Visitors can enjoy the scenic Wichita Mountains, and historic Greek and Gothic Revival-style architecture, and experience life in the 1880s during spring and fall encampments celebrating Lawton-Fort Sill's rich history.

Oklahoma's only university with a statewide presence, Oklahoma State University is a five-campus, public land-grant educational system working to improve people's lives in Oklahoma and the world through instruction, research and outreach. Established in 1890, OSU boasts students from all 50 states and 120 nations, and more than 200,000 alumni worldwide.

The college shares a rich heritage with our great state, from the seeds of knowledge sown on the Oklahoma prairie by OU's first president, David Ross Boyd, to President David L. Boren's *Reach for Excellence* campaign. We honor state legacy as we engineer a bright future through talented engineering graduates, new knowledge and technological innovation.

For more than a quarter century, Oklahoma doctors have turned to Physicians Liability Insurance Company (PLICO) for professional liability insurance coverage. Managed *by* physicians *for* physicians, PLICO is an outspoken advocate for the advancement of Oklahoma healthcare and is passionate about patient safety—two time-honored traditions that we will proudly continue throughout the 21st century.

UNIT CORPORATION®

Unit Corporation, a diversified energy company headquartered in Tulsa, Oklahoma, operates principally in the Mid-Continent region, including the Anadarko, Arkoma, Permian, Rocky Mountains and Gulf Coast Basins. The company specializes in exploration, acquisition and production of oil and natural gas, contract drilling of onshore oil and natural gas wells, and the gathering and processing of natural gas.

Founded in 1945 in Oklahoma City, W&W Steel has become one of the country's largest steel fabricating companies. With more than 1,100 employees and over 2 million square feet of production facilities in eight states, W&W Steel provides complete turnkey design, fabrication, and erection for domestic and international construction projects.

Williams, through its subsidiaries, primarily finds, produces, gathers, processes and transports natural gas. Williams' operations are concentrated in the Pacific Northwest, Rocky Mountains, Gulf Coast, Southern California and Eastern Seaboard.

CONTRIBUTING SPONSORS

Larry and Joyce Anderson

Aven Gas & Oil, Inc.

Steve and Lynn Biddle
McDonald's Restaurants, Enid

Bruce Boehs
Farmers and Merchants National Bank, Fairview

Michael D. & Tamara Oxley Brown
Resilient Corporation

Paul Bruce
AMVEST Osage, Inc.

Don and Lynda Cheatham

The First National Bank & Trust Co., Chickasha

James F. Consedine, II
Benefit Plan Strategies

Frank & Sally Deatherage

J. Scott Dickman

Dan and Kay Dillingham

Ken Fergeson
NBC "People You Can Bank ON"

Dr. Franklin and Judy Forney

Frankfurt-Short-Bruza Associates, P.C.

John D. and Virginia G. Groendyke

Rick and Lisa Hart
21 Ranch, Inc.

Stephen J. Heyman

Kent and Barbara Houck
Houck Agency

Gary and Connie Hulse

Marilyn Humphrey

Indian Electric Cooperative

Brent & Jennifer Kisling

Gary W. Lewis
Lamamco Drilling

Mark Lisle
Citizens Bank of Edmond

Ron Lukenbaugh
Mid-America Wholesale

Gregory L and Karen Mahaffey
Mahaffey & Gore, P.C.

Kirk Martin and John Beebe

Hoyt P. Mayes
First American Bank, Norman

David and Stephanie Meara

National Center for Employee Development
USPS

George Redwine, OD
Associated Optometrists of Oklahoma, Inc.

Carl Renfro
Pioneer Bank and Trust

Brad Shepherd

Dr. Brian and Susan Shewey

Dr. Roy Troutt

Lew O. Ward
Ward Petroleum Corp.

FRIENDS

Sandra Abbas
Gerald Adams
Don and Dot Adkins
Kelly Ailey
Steve and Katie Alcorn
Mike and Lori Alderman
Greg D. Allen
Harold and Phyllis Allen
Carroll and Laura Allison
Eldon Ames
Gary and Jackie Anderson
Janet Rogers Anderson
Joe and Julie Anderson
Leigh A. Anderson
Robert E. and Pat Anderson
Bill and Darla Andrew
In memory of Rob Andrew
Jarvis Annis
Melanie Anthony
Pauline Arnes
Brian and Sue Arnold
Aaron Arterburn
Bob and Jan Arterburn
Bill, Linda and Pam Athey
Diane Athey
Gary and Johnnie Atwood
Brett Austin
Jon Ax
Charles Bacon
Mr. and Mrs. Burck Bailey
Anella Baker
Lindy and Connie Baker
Paul and Nikki Baker
Margaret Bales
The Mathew Balkman Family
Thad and Amy Balkman
Agnes Ball
Frank Baker and Carmen Ball
Bank of Commerce, Duncan
Karen Barger
Dan and Peggy Barney
Mary French Barrett
Ron and Susan Bartlett
Terry Baxter
Berlinda Ann Bazzell
Mary Beach
Kent and Elizabeth Beaty
Wilma Beaty
Bill Becher
Wayne and Doris Bell
Mark and Lorna Benkendorf
Scott and Lynne Benkendorf
Gary and Audra Bennett
Bill Benton
Mike and Teresa Benway
John and Debbie Berg
Tom Berlie
Eli and Angelica Berry
Becky Best
Jody Biggers
Rick and Marsha Billings
Steve and Shelly Blair
Dr. Jerry and Mrs. Carolynne Blankenship
Roy Bliss
Jean Bobrinski
Jeanne Boese
Dean and Dixie Bomholt

David and Trina Bostwick
Don and Becky Bostwick
Eddie and Dian Bowen
John and Susan Bowers
Jack C. "Cory" Bowker
Alan, Polly, Emma and Connor Boyer
Larry and Kathy Boyer
Rick and Janet Bracher
Worth and Dorothy Bracher
Martha L. Brady
Steve, Kelly, Michaela, Lyndee and Kaylyn Branen
Zora Braun
Gary Brawner
Harold Brawner
Bill and Theresa Britt
Norman and Artie Britt
Kirbie Brittain
Rod and Joni Brittain
Spencer Brittain
Bill and Janell Brock
Bob and Mary Brooks
David and Lauren Brown
John Brown
Gary and Patti Brown
Doris Broyles
LeAnne Forney Brubaker
Marlene Buck
Lance and Cate Buckley
Frank Budd
Patsy Bugg
Marvin H. Bules
Bryan and Kris Bundy
Everet and Mary Burdick
Cary and Teri Burghardt
Alexzander Thomas Burns
Jim C. Burns
Maggie Burns
Mark Timothy Burns
Patrick Joseph Burns
Thomas John and Rita Irene Burns
Thomas Kevin Burns
David and April Burrows
Rachel, Liam and Stella Burton
Dr. Roy and Janet Camp
Ross and Sherry Campbell
Ann Grace Carey
Linda Rogers Carleton
Rosemary Carlyle
Carmen Public Library
Jack and June Carpenter
Phil and Ruth Carson
Michelle Carter
Charles W. Casey
Jennifer Casteel
Dave and Sue Chael
Don and Peggy Chambers
John and Lindy Chambers
Dr. Letitia Chambers
Stephen and Mary Suzan Chambers
Dr. Wade Chambers
Dixie Chapman
Edward Chapman
Overton M. "Buck" and Helen Cheadle
Lane and Jane Chenoweth
Jim and Beth Chestnut
Citizens Bank and Trust Co. of Ardmore
Claremore Reveille Rotary
Linda Clark
Sharon Clark
Coleman and Barbara Claypole
Joe and Connie Claypole

Clemon and Rita Clewell
Worrall and Jane Lee Clift
Bernice Clingenpeel
Kent and Terri Clingenpeel
Dennis, Anita and Kaci Clippinger
Philip and Terrie Clover
Jo Clow
James Cochran
Liz Cochrane
J. Stuart Cole
Bill Coleman
Clement D. Collogan
Holly and Bobby Conway
Joan Rogers Compton
Arda Cook
Agnes Cooper
Harold Cooper
Rick and Lerri Cooper
Clint and Jaquita Corley
Ron and Cynthia Corley
Jerry L. Cornelius
Kayle Costello
J. Ellen Cotton
J.L. and Elaine Courtney
John and Gene Covington
Jeff Cowan
Dustin and Demetra Cox
Howard Crain
Stacy Cramer
Chuck and Eilene Crites
Brent and Pat Crouse
Kenneth and Elena Cubbage
Ken Culver
Jackie H. Dahle
Jim and Harriet Davis
Kenny and Gina Davis
Lawrence Davis
Steve and Annette Davis
Tim DeClerck
Del City Kiwanis
Mr. and Mrs. Gordon Demerson
David Stuart den Daas
Don and Judy den Daas
Kathryn Paige den Daas
Denistry for Today, PC
Bob Dense
Darren and Heather Trecek DePalma
Dustin, Wendi and Pepper DeVaughn
Richard and Judy DeVaughn
Stephen DeVaughn
W.D. and Pat Diehl
Dr. Matt and Drue Diesselhorst
Peter and Annie Dillingham
Karissa Divelbiss
Keaton Divelbiss
Kenli Divelbiss
Kenny and Kristi Divelbiss
Kylen Divelbiss
KyOnda Divelbiss
Bryan and Margaret Dixon
N.J. and Lois Dixon
Jim and Mary Dobson
Jim and Nancy Dobson
Ann Dohrmann
Mary Lee Hert Draper
Chad, Meredith and Charlie Duke
Dayna Duke
Kyle Duncan
Paul and Lois Duncan
Charles and J. Dunkerley-Maupin
Rodney and Cecilia Dunkin

Steve and Wanda Dupy
Clarence and Joyce Durheim
Lila Dustin
Mick Dustin
Jeannie Ebersole
Bill and Donna Edson
George Leonard Edwards
Phil and Susie Edwards
Sarah "Kate" Edwards
Susie Edwards
Phil and Susan Elliott
Debbie Else
Jan Emo
Emrick's Van and Storage Co.
Enid High School - Class of 1947
Enid High School - Class of 1972
Enid Public Library
Judge Joe Enos
Henry Enterline
Roger and Sharlotte Epps
James and Barbara Erickson
Ed and Barbara Eskridge
Eskridge Lexus of Oklahoma City
Cara Jane Evans
Christa Evans
Nancy Evans
Patricia P. Evans
Rick and Virginia Evans
Tom and Cheryl Evans
Fairview City Library
Fairview Friends of the Library
Patrick Farrell
Richard and Linda Farris
Robert R. Faulk
Clyde and GiGi Faulkner
David Feisal
Rod Felber
John and Tricia Felt
Laura Fenton
Marsha Ferrier
Dr. Brad Fielding
Lynn File
Ed and Julie Fillinger
Brad, Jennifer, Megan, Haylee and Kaci Firgard
First National Bank, Okmulgee and Henryetta
Richard and Susan Q. Fitzgerald
Gary and Judy Fleming
Zane and Ann Fleming
Doug and Colleen Flikeid
Joe and Avis Forbes
Gay Lynn Forney
John and Tabitha Fothergill
Tim and Denice Fothergill
Tony and Keri Fothergill
Bettie S. Fousel
Carolyn Fowler
Dan Fox, Jr.
Robert Frakes
Summer Frame
Gary, Stefanie and Ian Franklin
Doug and Dianne Frantz
Don Frazier
Bill and Dora Lu Freeman
Steve and Rebecca Freeman
Lyle Fry
Bruce and Sherri Fuksa
Chloe, Ellie and in memory of Jake Fuksa
Tom and Kelly Funderburk
Chuck and Margaret Gall

Bill and Francesca Garner
Jody Garrett-Burns
Allyson Scott Gevertz
Paul and Mickie Giberson
Joyce Gilbert
Lonnie and Elsie Gillespie
Rob, Lynn and Hannah Gilstrap
Marlin G. "Ike" Glass, Jr.
Larry Gober
Mary Goetz
Donna Galyon Goff
Rebecca, Ron and Alexis Golden
Debby Goodman
Frankie Goodman
Tia Goodman
Todd Goodman
Jim and Peggy Goodrich
Sharon B. Goodwin
Cindy Gorrell
Gus and Pat Gray
Phillip and Donna Gray
Wess and Jolene Gray
Betty Green
Dennis Green
Mr. and Mrs. John Ray Green
Bob and Joyce Greenhaw
Bill and Judy Gregory
Cindy Griesel
Molly Levite Griffis
Mark and Genese Gunter
Adrian Hale
Hal and Sandra Hall
Lisa Hall
James Hammond
Dr. Michael Hampton
Roland and Kathy Haney
Charles Harding
Lou Hargrave
Eugene and Bertha Harraman
Ken and Jennifer Harraman
Jack Harrel
Bill and Pat Harris
Dan and Colleen Harris
Jim and Peggy Harris
Harrison and Mecklenburg, Inc.
Drs. Clanton and Selby Ann Harrison and family
Amelia Clay Hart
Daniel Wilson Hart
Becky Hatton
Timmy Hawley
Glen and Kathy Haworth
Jon and Tara Haworth
Louise Hazlette
Randy Heckenkemper
Bill and Karen Heizer
Warren and Nancy Hempfling
Bonnie Henderson
Shirley Hensley
Lynn and Leona Bennett Henson
Marietta Davis Henson
Sue Pilgrim Henthorn
Hewitt Mineral Corporation
Karen Hey-Harden
Amy Hiatt
Beth Hightower
Byron and Sara Hill
Cynthia Hilterbrand
Jim and Phyllis Hilton
Myron Hilton
Alan Hoad
Fran and Martha Hoad

Raymond Hoad
Bill and Carla Hobbs
Rae E. Hoddy
Bob and Mary Jo Hoffman
Harold T. and Edna Mae Holden
Tim and Allison Holden
Deborah Holle
Michael and Teri Holle
Penny Holt
Rob and Lavon Holtzinger
Gary and Barbara Hook
Lori Hopkins
Dick and Denise Hopper
Don and Doris Hopper
Martha Horn
Curtis and Thelma Horrall
Jim and Lynn Howard
Kevin D. and Patty O. Howard
Donald and Louise Howe
Julia, Katherine and William Huckaby
David and Leslie Hughes
Monte and Laura Humphrey
Todd and Cindy Humphrey
John and Trish Hunter
John and Jennifer Hurd
Farhat Husain, M.D. and
Larry C. Hazelwood
George A. Hutchinson
Bob and Nancy Inselman
Penni Ivy
Bill and Elaine Jackson
Carroll and Shirley Jackson
Ron and Betsy Jacobs
Richard and Patsy James
Holly Jamin
Colleen Jantzen
Drs. Grant and Jennifer Janzen
Carole Jeffries
David and Martha Johnson
Rev. Don and Tary Davis Johnson
Randal Johnson
Rob and Sharla Johnson
Roe and Billie Johnson
Tom and Cheri Johnson
Germaine Johnston
Bruce and Ann Jones
Eva Jones
Jay and Tava Jones
Valerie Jones
Mary June Bumgarner Joseph
Ralph and Barbara Joslin
Terri Joslin
Robin Karns
Christopher and Andra Keim
Linda Montgomery Keleher
Edward F. and Marilyn Keller
Frank and Lucy Kenslow
Arnold and Sharon Kenyon
Judy Kidd
Darcy Fox Kidwell
Barbara Kimbrough
Dr. Larry and Kay Kiner
Dewey and Betty Lou King
Joe and Peggy King
Paul King
Tom and Claudia King
William J. King
Dayna Kinkaid
Dale and Bobby Kirkpatrick
Judith Kirton
Kim Kirton

Frank and Annabelle Kisling
Brett and Lindsey Klemme
Hunter Allen Klemme
Kaitlyn Dawn Klemme
Paige Klemme
Robert L. "Bob" Klemme
Suzanne Bracher Klemme
Roy Knapp
Barry and Irene Knight
John A. and Carol Knuppel
Mary Ann Koehn
Paula Kramer
Michael Krywucki
Bob and Charlotte Kummell
Eric Kurtz
Barbara LaFrance
Jim and Margaret Lambke
Jeff and Dawn Langlinais
Sherry Lankford
Gene Lathrop
Dr. Charles Lawrence
Jeff and Claire Lawrence
Lawton Chapter of AMBUCS
Dennis Ledbetter
Celia A. Lehmann
Alyne Lewallen
Jeanette Lewis
Jim and Jean Lewis
John and Letha Lieb
Larry and Jennifer Liggett
Judge Dean and Wylodean Linder
Roger and Alta Linthicum
Joe and Nancy Litsch
Billie Little
Leonard M. Logan IV
Rick and Patti Long
Gene Lowery
Congressman Frank D. Lucas
Joy Lugar
O. Dolores Lukenbaugh
Robert and Mary Etta Lukenbaugh
Ron Lukenbaugh
Rob and Barbara Lund
Laverne Lundy
Tri Luong
Jim and Betsy Mabry
Steve Mackey
John G. Madden II
John G. Madden IV and family
Doug and JoAnne Mahaffey
Robert M. and Debbie Mahaffey
Steve and Virginia Mahaffey
Sylvia G. Mahoney
Sara Malone
Gary Mannies
Chris and Lori Markes
Derek S. Marsh
Barry T. Marsh
David Martens
Joel and Darlene Martin
John and Nancy Martin
Linda Mason
David and Nancy May
Mel and Bonnie May
Randy and Susan Mayberry
Lee Mayfield
Buddy and Valerie McCamey
Larry and Dolores McClure
Mike McCool
Ron McDonald
Frances McGrew

Mary McGuire
Ted A. McGuire
Clark McKeever
Brad and LaDonna McKinzie
Dick and Lavonn McKnight
Betty Gene McMahan
In Memory of John L. McMahan
Chris, Regina and Ryleigh McNabb
James, Nita and Patrick McPartland
Jill Forney McPherson
John D. Meara
Michael Paul Meara
Medford Public Library
Brenda K. Messenger
Marty and Shannon Meyer
Morgan Jane Meyer
Payton Mecate Meyer
Karl L. Meyers
Harry Millard
Don and Georgia Miller
Dr. Joe and Liz Miller
Mike and Sandra Milligan
John and Susan Mitchell
Beverly Moery
Dan Montague
Jim and Sue Montgomery
Monty and Karen Moore
Walt and Jann Moore
Warren Moore
Gene and Pat Morahan
Gene and Bonnie Morgan
Polly Morgan
Tracy and Kay Morris
Norman Glass and Vera Morris
Jay and Louise Morrish
Roxi Morrissey
Scott and Hillarie Trecek Moseley
Richard D. "Rick" Mosier
Gene Mozingo
Jane Mudgett
Alexandra Munger
Garrison E. and Jane Munger
John Munger
Frank and Jan Munn
Larry Murphy
Craig Myers
Sydney Devynn Myers
Jeff and Jennifer Neal
Dale Neikirk
Hugh Hart Nelson
Ryan and Susan Nelson
David H. and Deborah C. Neuroth
Court and Rosalyn Newkirk
Steve and Barbara Newton
John and Sarah Nicholas
Nicholas Farm and Ranch
Warren Nicklas
Herb Niles
Richard E. and Dorothy Niles
Ken and Sue Nivens
Northcutt Chevrolet, Buick and Toyota
Leonard and Roxanne Northcutt
Scott, Christy and Nate Northcutt
Pat and Gail Novak
Gene and A.M. Nowlin
Richard and Joy Nowlin
D.J. and Melissa Nuzum
Della Ruth Nuzum
Don and Lori Nuzum
Jim and Dodie O'Brien
Michael, Anna, and Caroline O'Hare

Old Germany Restaurant
Harvey Olson
Dr. Dwight and Dianne Olson
Olson Animal Hospital
Ray and Linda Gayle Orf
Nell Outhier
Phil and Linda Outhier
Eldon Overstreet
Roy and Florence Oxford
Larry Pace and Co.
George W. Paczkowski
Feildon Parham
Ryon, Jennifer and Will Parham
Gib and Lauren Park
J.W. and Mary Jo Parker
Brenda Pate
Donna Patocka
Mitchell, Linda and Molly Payne
D.W. Perkins
Donnie and Sarah Perkins
Don and Ann Pettus
Don and Rose Peyton
Don and Teresa Peyton
Mr. and Mrs. Boyd D. Phillips
Lynn and Sally Phillips
Joe Phipps
Kathy Phipps
Dwayne and Connie Plowman
Andrea J. Potter
Mark E. Potter
Mary Ann Potter
Michael G. Potter
Ray H. Potter
John and Cherie Poyas
Licia Price
Norris and Betty Price
Patty Probasco
Dan and Marilyn Pryor
Vergie A. Pryor
Jim and Marilyn Pulliam
Thomas A. Quillin, Jr.
John and Frances Quinn
Eric Ragain
Bob and Joyce Ramer
Corey Raschen
Ed Raschen
Timi Raschen
Terry and Lorna Ratzlaff
Ruth Raupe
Dr. Prasad Reddy
Frederick Redwine
Phil and Sarah Redwine
Philip Redwine. Jr.
Ryan Redwine
Winnie Redwine
Fawn Reely
Mr. and Mrs. Carl F. Reherman
Allen and Pat Reid
Mark and LeAnn Reid
Krey and Krista Reimer
Vic, Marla, Stacia and Kristi Rempel
Republic Bank and Trust, Norman
Research Tax Consultants
Timothy and Debi Reynolds
Mark, Becky and Alisha Reynolds
Dr. Bob and Beverly Rice
Robin Richardson
Carlton and Arlene Riemer
David and Ann Ritchie
Jim and Ardis Rives
Bob and Mary Ann Robinson

Brittany Robinson
Brooks Robinson
Brynn Robinson
Don and Pam Robinson
Jeffrey B. Robinson
Ron and Eva Robinson
Randall and Carol Robison
Frank C. Robson
Nancy Roeming
Gene R. Rogers
Drs. James and Cindy Rogers
Robert Galyon Rogers
Robert L. Rogers
David Root
Robert L. Rorschach
Corwin and Harolyn Rose
Will Rosebure
Mr. and Mrs. Wayne E. Rowe, Jr.
Mike and Pam Ruby
Pat and Nancy Ruby
Steven and Lacy Ruby
Fred and Beverly Rupp
Maxine Russell
Hugh and Pat Sage
Samson Investment Company
Dr. Bruce C. Saxon and family
John H. Saxon III, M.D.
Dave and Tricia Schlittler and family
Teresa Schroeder
Ronald Schulz
Jack L. and Donna Scott
John and Marsha Scott
Andrew Scott and Rebecca
Delmar, Andrea, Caleb and Seth Scoville
Cliff and Janet Seifert
Tad Seifert, M.D.
Dr. David and Carolyn Selby
Diane Selph
Gene and Carolyn Semrad
Tillie Sewell
Glenn and Polly Sharp
Eugene and Shelly Sharp
Robert and Linda Shaver
Jayson, Brandon and Jeremy Shellady
Kathy Shellady
Rex and Dianne Shelton
Mr. and Mrs. Burt Sheriff
Mary Sherman
Bill and Jana Shewey
Drs. Jeff and Stacia Shipman
Jim and Cynthia Shipman
Dr. Robert and Betty Shuttee
Bruce and Cindy Simon
Lou and Diane Simpkins
David Singer
Bill and Jo Smith
Bill and Pat Smith
Dennis Smith
Earlene Heaton Smith
Edward and Sharon Smith
Harlan Smith
Kirk Smith
Lori Smith
Lynn and Lou Ann Smith
Pat Smith
Paul and Betty Smith
Steve Smith
Todd, Sheila and Samantha Smith
Vivian Smith
Judy Snell
Merrill Snider

Susan Southall
Shirley Spaeth
Arch Spencer
Daryle Spencer
Michael and Lainey Staires
Oral F. Stake
Jimmy and Abbey Stallings
Rob and Mary Stallings
Ross Stallings
Shaun and Kelli Stanley
Michael Stebens
Carolyn Steely
Alex and Esther Steinert
Colleen Stephenson
Emmy Scott Stidham
Cathy Stirewalt
Fred and Betty Stoabs
Ryan and Kristen Stoabs
Lisa Stone
Stanley and Bobbie Stoner
Lucy T. Storer
Jim and Sharon Strate
Jerry and Brenda Streck
Roberta Stuckey
William and Anne Sturdevant
Randall Sullivan
Dwayne Sumter
Richard and Cheryl Swanson
Alan and Lanell Taylor
Jeff and Alicia Taylor
John W. and Sue Taylor
Kathy Taylor
Mary Taylor
Michael and Sharon Taylor
Steve and Lori Taylor
Steve and Melanie Taylor
Tom and Betsy Taylor
The First National Bank and Trust Co., Newcastle
The Flintco Companies, Inc.
Lawrence and Thelma Theriot
Peter and Peggy Thies
Elgin E. Thomas
John and Linda Thomas
Paul and Melinda Thomas
Chuck Thompson
Steve and Susie Thornbrugh
Judge Norman Thygesen
Mary F. Tilford
William Tingler
Tobie Titsworth
David and Brenda Towe
Makenzie West Towe
Brad and Annessa Traynor
Dan and Amy Traynor
Tim and Suzy Traynor
Jim and Barbara Whiteis Trecek
John and Patty Trimmer
David and Sharon Trojan
Mr. and Mrs. Ernest J. Trojan
Rob and Megan Tsuyuki
Tom Tucker
Mike Turek
Deborah Turner
Turner Tours
Linda Tutwiler
Troy, Deb, Kaylene and Erin Ullom
Dwight and Luella Unruh
Mike and Kathryn Upchurch
Marianna Vance
Dennis and Mary Vance
Shannah VanHoose

Margaret Jenks VanHorn
Ricardo and Carey Sue Vega
Gary Vogel
Mike and Carol Wagar
Travis and Jill Wagar
Will and Meredith Wagar
John, Shelli, Eric and Lyndon Walke
Nadine Walterscheidt and family
Robin and Cydney Walvoord
Roy and Cherie Ward
Randy Waters
Watonga Public Library
Bob and Jean Watts
Jack and Betty Weber
Ted and Cheri Weber
Eric, Sarah and Jack Nathan Weisgarber
Paul and Sarah Welch
The Welch Family
Margy Weldon
Dr. James S. Wells
Robert Irvin and Judith Ann West
John and Edna Westmoreland
Elbert and Meme Wheeler
Evan and Karen Wheeler
Lon Franklin Whisler
Betty Harts Whitaker
Jane White
Kyle and Roxanne Whiteis
Mason Whiteis
Matt and Robin Whiteis
Mitchell Whiteis
Riley Whiteis
Robert and Sally Whiteneck
Rev. David Wiggs and Mary Hughes
Becky Wilber
Dane Wilber
Jeff and Patti Wilber
Phillip Wilber
Mike and Julie Ann Wiley
Brad and Jerri Williams
John and Bobby Lou Williams
Martha Williams
Myke and Kay Williams
Maggie Elizabeth Wilson
Lauren Wilson-McGeough
Dr. Bill Winans
In memory of Bobby Winans
Terry and Tina Winn
Chris and Jamie Wolff
Danny and Christi Wood
Cameron Joseph Wooden
Drs. Mark and Alexa Woodson
Corry and Beth Woolington
Sammie and Janis Wooten
Cyril and Virginia Wright
Jim and Maureen Wright
Margaret Wright
Meredith Wright
Tim and Janet Wright
The Yauk Family
Clark and Beth Young
Erlene Young
Steve and Lisa Youngquist
Dan and Brenda Zaloudek
Judy Zaloudek
Mick and Sue Zaloudek
Mr. and Mrs. Paul Ziegenfuss
Mary Sue Zimmermann
Dr. David and Sharla Zuech

SPECIAL THANKS

Louise Abercrombie
Ponca City News

Craig Adams
Clinton Rotary

Larry Adams
Kingfisher Rotary

Larry Anderson
Ditch Witch

David Arbour
Red Slough Wildlife Management Area

Sue Arnold
Cherokee Strip Bank Women

Ashley Arnold
KWTV

Phil Bacharach
Governor Brad Henry's Office

Frank Baker
Eagle Marketing

Jeff Barnes
Arbuckle Wilderness

Robert Barron
Enid News and Eagle

Sophia Befort
Enid Ambucs

Lynn Benkendorf
Eagle Marketing

Justin Berst
Chickasaw Nation

Roger Beverage
Oklahoma Bankers Association

Lynn and Steve Biddle
McDonald's Enid

Bob Blackburn
Oklahoma Historical Society

Jon Blankenship
Garfield County Development Alliance, Inc.

Brad Boeckman
Enid Ambucs

Geri Bonds
OKC Metro

Mike Brown
Community Publishers Inc.

Katrina Bryant
Great Western Trail Drive

Marlene Buck
OSU Cooperative Extension Service Enid

Jim Burnett
Western Enterprises

Ken Busby
Tulsa Arts and Humanities Council

Gary Caimano
Celebrate Productions, Inc.

Susan Camp
Duncan Rotary

Stuart Campbell
Little River Zoo

Phil Carson
Pilot (aerial photography)

Corey Cart
Lazy E Promotions

Lindy Chambers
Main Street Enid

Rebecca Chandler
Chickasaw Nation

Shane Claypool
ADM

Randy Cloud
OKC Ambucs

Jim Cobb
Cobb Engineering

Rodney Coe
The Clint Williams Company

Tim Colwell
Rotary Club Downtown Tulsa

Jim Consedine
Pilot (aerial photography)

Rick Cooper
W&W Steel Company

Ed Copelin
Norman Rotary Club

Melissa Craig
South Central Coal Company

Kathryn Crenweige
Weyerhaeuser

Galen Culver
KFOR

Todd Cunningham
Tulsa Ballet

Sheila Curley
Tulsa Chamber of Commerce

Valory Dalton
The Ford Center

Sandy Daniels
Chisholm Trail Broadcasting

Bob Davis
Guthrie Masonic Temple

Jacqi Davis
OK Mozart

Dale Day
Remington Park

Chuck Dehart
The Williams Companies

Travis Dennett
Bank of Vici

Kathy Dickson
Pawnee Bill Museum

Kristin Dotson
Celebrity Attractions

Penny Drennan
Keller Williams Broadcasting

Howard Evans
Balloon Pilot

Lynn Evans
Pilot (aerial photography)

Bob Farrell
Vance Air Force Base

Ken Fergeson
National Bank of Commerce

Scott Fitzgerald
Enid Morning News

Danna Fowble
The Oklahoma State Chamber of Commerce

Steve Frantz
Western Enterprises

Jerry Frech
Woodward Rotary

Chris Freet
OU Athletics

Jerry Glasgow
Guthrie

Steve Glime
American Airlines

Kara Hahn
Orange Peel

Scott Hall
OKC Hornets

Doug Hawthorne
Oklahoma International Bluegrass Festival

Molly Helm
Autry Technology Center

Edna Hennessee
Cosmetic Specialty Labs

Roland Herwig
Federal Aviation Association

Stephen Hillman
Tulsa Business Journal

Alisa Hines
Oklahoma Horizon

Edna MaeHolden
Enid

Kevin Hook
Community Newspapers

Heather Hope
Tulsa Opera

Mike Houck
OU Athletics

Debbie Humphrey
Omniplex

Keith Jackson
Lawton

Elaine Johns
Northwest Aero Services

Rob Johnson
Eagle Marketing

Brenda Johnson
Oklahoma State Capitol

David Keathly
The Marland Estate

Karen Keith
Tulsa Convention and Visitors Bureau

Emily Kelley
Fort Sill Public Relations

Randy Kersey
Dell City Kiwanis

Brent Kisling
United States Department of Agriculture

Jay Lakin
OKC Blazers

Jim Langdon
Langdon Publishing

Del Langham
PLICO

Del Langham
PLICO

Sherry Lankford
Shawnee News-Star

Shelia Lee
Lawton Chamber of Commerce

Loren Liebscher
P_Bar Farms

John Little
Enid Rotary

Ba T. Luong
Super Cao Nguyen

Marcie Mack
Autry Technology Center

Jay Martin
Martin Bionics

Debra Martin
OETA

Jim Mason
Oklahoma Nano Technology Initiative

Rob McClendon
Oklahoma Horizon

Lou Meibergen
Johnston Enterprises, Inc.

Brian Meyer
Enid Lions Club

Kathy Montgomery
Guthrie Chamber of Commerce

Kenny Mossman
OU Athletics

Court Newkirk
Lawton Chamber of Commerce

Mike Noteware
OSU Athletics

Jeanne Oden
Ackerman-McQueen

Eric Oesch
Red Earth

Leslie Paris
Bank of Oklahoma

Randa Parrish
Prairie Quilt

Ron Patton
Pauls Valley Rotary

Tim Paul
Bama Companies

Tracy Perkins
Northwest Aero Services

Jessica Pfau
Ardmore Rotary

Betty Price
Oklahoma Arts Council

Renee Punch
Unit Corporation

Donald Pyeatt
Shawnee Rotary

Anna Redaelli
Elk City Rotary

Alan Reed
Enid Ambucs

Ron Robinson

Judy GibbsRobinson
The Daily Oklahoman

Stephanie Royse
Fred Jones Jr. Museum of Art

Mike Ruby
OG&E

Dick Rush
The Oklahoma State Chamber of Commerce

Andy Schwab
Braum's

David Scott
Oklahoma City Will Rogers Airport

Shane and Sara Scribner
Scribner's Gallery

Gary Shutt
Oklahoma State University

Larry Skoch
Oklahoma Living Magazine

Connie Smedley
Broken Arrow Library

Bruce Stallsworth
Oklahoma Independent Petroleum Association

Kevin Stark
The Toy and Action Figure Museum

Joanie Stephenson
Steve's Sundries

Stan Stoner
Stoner Advertising

Dr. Jim Strate
Autry Technology Center

Shelley Stutchman
Enid AM Ambucs

Brenda Thornton
Equal Opportunity and Workforce Diversity

Jim Thrash
Oklahoma City Will Rogers Airport

Donald Tomkalski
Tulsa University

David Towe
Lawton Ambucs

Patricia Tramel
OU School of Engineering

Blake Wade
Oklahoma Centennial Commission

T.L. Walker
Standing Bear Native American Foundation

Jenny Wallace
Field's Pecan Pies

Earlene Washburn
Claremore Rotary

Hardy Watkins
Oklahoma Department of Tourism

Judy Watson
Enid Ambucs

Amy Weaver
Oklahoma Centennial Commission

Kyle Whiteis
Auto Crane Company

Bobby Willis
Teacup Chain Square Dancing Club

Michelle Winters
OKC Philharmonic

Heston Wright
Weatherford Rotary

Connie Yellowman
Red Earth

Doug Yoder
Mustang Rotary

Dan Zaloudek

No thank-you list is ever perfect. I deeply appreciate all others not mentioned here who contributed in any way to the success of this project.
— Mike Klemme

CELEBRATING OKLAHOMA!
THE OKLAHOMA CENTENNIAL PHOTOGRAPHIC SURVEY

Photographer and Editor-in-Chief
Mike Klemme

Executive Editor
Rick Long

Managing Editor
Sarah J. West

Graphic Designer
Brian Burton

Contributing Writers
Kate Edwards
Jennifer Huckaby
Kathy Murphy
Michael Staires

Web Developer
Dave Schlittler

Director of Business Development
Jim Trecek

Photo Archivist
Margaret Wright

Director of Finance
Suzanne Klemme

ADDITIONAL PHOTO CREDITS

p. 74 ...... Fred Jones Jr. Museum of Art,
Courtesy of Robert H. Taylor

p. 78 ...... Tulsa Ballet Performance of "Swan Lake,"
Courtesy of Christopher Jean-Richard

p. 105 ..... Courtesy of Guthrie Scottish Rite
of Freemasonry

p. 123 ..... Courtesy of United States Postal Service
National Center for Employee Development

p. 162 ..... Coleman Theatre Beautiful, Courtesy of
Gary Crowe

p. 165 ..... Courtesy of Remington Park

p. 166 ..... Courtesy of University of Tulsa Football

PHOTO INDEX

Three More Ways to Celebrate!

Many of the beautiful photographs in *Celebrating Oklahoma!* are available for purchase as **fine art prints**. Bring the spirit of Oklahoma into your home or office.

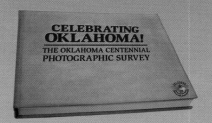

Order an extra copy of the Special Edition or the Collectors Edition of our historic *Celebrating Oklahoma!* **coffee table book** for yourself, or as a gift for a loved one or business associate.

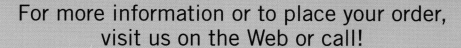

Businesses and organizations should also take note of our **Custom Corporate Program.** It's the perfect promotional vehicle for dynamic, civic-minded enterprises.

Your company photo could be here!

For more information or to place your order, visit us on the Web or call!

www.celebratingoklahoma.com

1.800.338.1656

END PAGES: Detail, Oklahoma granite with lichens and moss